ISBN 978-0-260-10393-2
PIBN 10928215

For support please visit www.forgottenbooks.com

A MONTHLY SCIENCE JOURNAL
37TH YEAR—ESTABLISHED 1956

Last Call for Abstracts
1992 OPEN FORUM
Deadline is June 6

- Chest Physical Therapy: Time for a Redefinition and a Renaming

- A New Journal Feature—Kittredge's Corner: Technical Aspects of Respiratory Care

- Effect of Nebulizer Position on Aerosol Delivery during MV

- Flow Resistance in Adult Manual Resuscitators

- Predicting Academic Success in a 4-Year Program

- MDI Gas Volumes at Three Levels of Canister Fullness

- Points of View: Patient-Focused Hospitals

OW TO BUILD
AMERICA'S #1
EAK FLOW METER
IN 10 EASY STEPS

1. cons

We st
other peak f
the leader. w
selves. In th
made more t
improvemen
on the draw

2. Dev

ASS
use a unique
that minimi
accuracy, re
How consist
lated daily u
research stu
1% variabili

1. Nurture a drive to constantly be better

We started out competing against other peak flow meters. Now that we're the leader, we compete against ourselves. In the last two years alone, we've made more than 10 separate product improvements...with more still on the drawing boards.

2. Develop a patented design

ASSESS® and ASSESS Low Range use a unique flow-sampling technology that minimizes wear and delivers superior accuracy, reproducibility, and consistency. How consistent? After two years of simulated daily use, a recent independent research study found no more than 1% variability.[1]

3. Engineer it without compromise

Everything about ASSESS from its easy-to-use design...to its easy-to-read scale...to its transparent construction that encourages regular cleaning...to its virtually indestructible polycarbonate body—is designed to make it work better and last longer.

4. Test every unit

Spot-checking is the norm in manufacturing quality control. Not at HealthScan. *No* unit leaves our plant without being tested at both the high and low ends of the scale. (Plus, every hour we select ten random samples for even more rigorous statistical quality control.)

5. Put it to the test in the laboratory

Recently, researchers at Montefiore Medical Center measured ASSESS against our leading competitor. Their findings? The accuracy of the other product deteriorated after only two months of simulated use. But ASSESS kept on delivering consistently accurate readings.[2]

6. Put it to the test in clinical practice

Lab results like this say a lot about ASSESS. Our clinical acceptance says even more. Nine out of every ten peak flow meters used in hospitals are ASSESS.[1] Why? Read on.

7. Support physicians

Physicians know they can count on us, not just for a superior product but for superior service—including extensive patient education materials, a dedicated professional services department, and the only comprehensive peak flow monitoring system.

8. Support patients and their families

We don't *have* to donate hundreds of units every year to asthma camps across America. Or back ASSESS with an *unlimited* one-year warranty. Or make a special Braille unit for blind patients. Or provide patient instructions in other languages. We just figure it's the responsibility of a leader.

9. Invite criticism

With all these efforts, you might think we'd hate to hear complaints about ASSESS. Just the opposite. Frank feedback from physicians and patients only helps us make ASSESS better. Which is why we encourage that feedback with a toll-free telephone hotline.

10. Go back to step 1

We're proud of our leadership... but we're not satisfied. So we'll keep on making improvements. We expect more of ASSESS. You should too.

For more information—or to order ASSESS for your practice—call toll-free **1-800-962-1266.**

ASSESS® Peak Flow Meter

STANDARD RANGE	LOW RANGE
60 to 880 L/min	30 to 390 L/min

Setting the standard for peak flow monitoring.

References: 1. Data on file, HealthScan Products Inc., 2. Shapiro S, Hendler J, Ogirala R, et al.: An evaluation of the accuracy of Assess and MiniWright peak flowmeters. Chest 99;358-362. 1991.
ASSESS and ASSESS Low Range meet *National Asthma Education Program Technical Standards for Peak Flow Meters,* January, 1991. AA710001-0 10/91

HealthScan Products Inc., 908 Pompton Avenue, Cedar Grove, NJ 07009-1292

RE/PIRATORY CARE

A Monthly Science Journal. Established 1956. Official Journal of the American Association for Respiratory Care.

EDITORIAL OFFICE
11030 Ables Lane
Dallas TX 75229
(214) 243-2272

EDITOR
Pat Brougher RRT

ADJUNCT EDITOR
Philip Kittredge RRT

EDITORIAL COORDINATOR
Donna Stephens BBA

EDITORIAL BOARD
Neil R MacIntyre MD, Chairman
Thomas A Barnes EdD RRT
Richard D Branson RRT
Robert L Chatburn RRT
Charles G Durbin Jr MD
Thomas D East PhD
Dean Hess MEd RRT
Robert M Kacmarek PhD RRT
David J Pierson MD
James K Stoller MD

CONSULTING EDITORS
Frank E Biondo BS RRT
Howard J Birenbaum MD
John G Burford MD
Bob Demers BS RRT
Douglas B Eden BS RRT
Donald R Elton MD
Robert R Fluck Jr MS RRT
Ronald B George MD
James M Hurst MD
Charles G Irvin PhD
MS Jastremski MD
Hugh S Mathewson MD
Michael McPeck BS RRT
Richard R Richard BS RRT
John Shigeoka MD
R Brian Smith MD
Jack Wanger RCPT RRT
Jeffrey J Ward MEd RRT

JOURNAL ASSOCIATES
Stephen M Ayres MD
Reuben M Cherniack MD
Joseph M Civetta MD
John B Downs MD
Donald F Egan MD
Gareth B Gish MS RRT
George Gregory MD
Ake Grenvik MD
H Frederick Helmholz Jr MD
John E Hodgkin MD
William F Miller MD
Ellan J Nelson RN RRT
Thomas L Petty MD
Alan K Pierce MD
Henning Pontoppidan MD
John W Severinghaus MD
Barry A Shapiro MD

PRODUCTION STAFF
Linda Barcus
Steve Bowden
Donna Knauf
Jeannie Marchant

CONTENTS

May 1992
Volume 37, Number 5

SIEMENS

Introducing a precision wind instrument that's in tune with the future...

The new Servo Ventilator 300. With a totally new functional design that's setting the tone for ventilatory management for years to come.

Unique composition...
Component flexibility allows you to configure the system conveniently, so the operating controls are always within easy reach, for easy reference.

Fine tuning...
A user friendly tutorial actually guides you in setting all the required operating parameters for improved time and accuracy.

Upscale selections...
Let it take you beyond the routine. Selections include two new ventilation modalities to help meet today's challenges in adult, pediatric and neonatal patient care.

Future performances...
Truly upgradeable, this future-friendly system will expand to accommodate additional hardware and software updates as they develop—to keep you out in front. Technologically. Clinically.

Our new focus is tuned to meeting your needs and your patient's needs in ventilator care.

To learn more about the revolutionary new Servo Ventilator 300 or for a personal demonstration, contact your local Siemens representative.

Siemens Medical Systems, Inc.
Patient Care Systems Division
10 Constitution Avenue
Piscataway, NJ 08855
Toll-Free 1-800-944-9046

Siemens...
technology in caring hands.

Circle 130 on reader service card

MANUSCRIPT SUBMISSION
Instructions for Authors and Typists is printed near the end of RESPIRATORY CARE on a quarterly basis (Jan, Apr, July, Nov).

PHOTOCOPYING & QUOTATION
PHOTOCOPYING. Any material in this journal that is copyrighted by Daedalus Enterprises, Inc may be photocopied for noncommericial purposes of scientific or educational advancement.

QUOTATION. Anyone may, without permission, quote up to 500 words of material in this journal that is copyrighted by Daedalus Enterprises Inc, provided the quotation is for noncommercial use, and provided RESPIRATORY CARE is credited. Longer quotation requires written approval by the author and publisher.

SUBSCRIPTIONS/CHANGES OF ADDRESS
RESPIRATORY CARE
11030 Ables Lane
Dallas TX 75229
(214) 243-2272

SUBSCRIPTIONS. Individual subscription rates are $50.00 per year (12 issues) in the U.S. and Puerto Rico, $70.00 per year in all other countries; $95.00 for 2 years in the U.S. and Puerto Rico, $135.00 in all other countries; and $140 for 3 years in the U.S. and Puerto Rico, $200.00 in all other countries (add $84.00 per year for air mail). Annual organizational subscriptions are offered to members of associations according to their membership enrollment as follows: 101-500 members—$5.00. 501-1,500 members—$4.50, 1,501-2,500 members—$4.25, 2,501-5,000 members—$4.00, 5,001-10,000 members—$3.00, and over 10,000 members—$2.50. Single copies, when available, cost $5.00; add $7.00 air mail postage to overseas countries.

CHANGE OF ADDRESS. Six weeks notice is required to effect a change of address. Note your subscription number (from the mailing label) your name, and both old and new address, including zip codes. Please note your subscription number on the envelope. Copies will not be replaced without charge unless request is received within 60 days of the mailing in the U.S. or within 90 days in other countries.

MARKETING DIRECTOR
Dale Griffiths

ADVERTISING ASSISTANT
Beth Binkley

ADVERTISING. Display advertising should be arranged with the advertising representatives. RESPIRATORY CARE does not publish a classified advertising column.

ADVERTISING: RATES & MEDIA KITS
Aries Advertising Representatives
Saul Hornik
Sandy Getterman
Diana Bacic
4 Orchard Hill Road
Marlboro NJ 07746
(908) 946-1224
fax (908) 946-1229

CONTENTS, *Continued*

May 1992
Volume 37, Number 5

Abstracts | Summaries of Pertinent Articles in Other Journals

---

Editorials, Statements, and Reviews To Note

Airway Considerations in the Management of Patients Requiring Long-Term Endotracheal Intubation (Review)—DJ Stone and DL Bogdonoff. Anesth Analg 1992;74:276-287.

Safety and Efficacy of Theophylline in Children with Asthma (Special Article)—L Hendeles, M Weinberger, S Szefler, and E Ellis. J Pediatr 1992;120:177.

Medical Problems Associated with Underwater Diving (Review)—Y Melamed, A Shupak, and H Bitterman. N Engl J Med 1992;326:30-35.

Thoracic Complications of Extracorporeal Membrane Oxygenation: Findings on Chest Radiographs and Sonograms—GW Gross, J Cullen, MS Kornhauser, PJ Wolfson. Am J Radiol 1992;158:353. (See Page 410 of this journal.)

The 'Cuff-Leak' Test for Extubation—MMcD Fisher, RF Raper. Anaesthesia 1992;47:10.

The 'cuff-leak' test, which involves demonstrating a leak around a tracheal tube with the cuff deflated, has been advocated to determine the safety of extubation in patients with upper airway obstruction. In 62 such patients we were able safely to extubate all patients with a cuff leak. Two patients extubated without cuff leak required reintubation and in 5 patients who repeatedly failed the test, tracheostomy was performed. Subsequently, we extubated 10 patients who were stable on spontaneous ventilation and did not have cuff leak; 3 later required tracheostomy and 7 were uneventfully extubated. While the presence of cuff leak demonstrates that extubation is likely to be successful, a failed cuff-leak test does not preclude uneventful extubation and if used as a criterion for extubation may lead to unnecessarily prolonged intubation or to unnecessary tracheostomy.

Preoxygenation in Children: For How Long?—RLR Videira, PPR Neto, RV Gomide Do Amaral, JA Freeman. Acta Anaesthesiol Scand 1992;36:109.

Although preoxygenation has been extensively studied, to our knowledge this is the first study addressing its optimal length in children, who form a high risk group for developing hypoxaemia during induction of anaesthesia. Recommended preoxygenation times in children range between 1 and 4 min, but whether one of these times maintains arterial oxygen saturation (S_aO_2) at an adequate level for a longer time period is unknown. This study was performed on 11 healthy children, randomly distributed into either Group 1 (1 min of preoxygenation, n = 6) or Group 2 (3 min of preoxygenation, n = 5). S_aO_2 was measured by pulse oximetry. While the patients were breathing room air, S_aO_2 was similar in both groups (97%) and rose to 100% after preoxygenation in all patients. After intravenous induction of anaesthesia

and muscle relaxation, all patients became apnoeic. The time taken for the S_aO_2 to decrease to 90% was measured. In Group 1 this occurred in 91 s, whereas Group 2 required 144 s. Thus, a 3-min rather than a 1-min period of preoxygenation would appear to maintain S_aO_2 at a safe level for a longer time in children.

Validity of a Disposable End-Tidal CO_2 Detector in Verifying Endotracheal Tube Placement in Infants and Children—MS Bhende, AE Thompson, DR Cook, AL Saville. Ann Emerg Med 1992;21:142.

STUDY OBJECTIVE: To examine the validity of a disposable, colorimetric end-tidal CO_2 detector in verifying endotracheal tube (ETT) placement in infants and children. DESIGN: The detector was studied prospectively in 151 intubations. SETTING: Operating room, ICU, and emergency department of a children's hospital. PARTICIPANTS: 137 children undergoing endo-

BRIEF SUMMARY: Please see package insert for full prescribing information.

SURVANTA® (1040)
beractant
intratracheal suspension

Sterile Suspension/For Intratracheal Use Only

INDICATIONS AND USAGE
SURVANTA is indicated for prevention and treatment ("rescue") of Respiratory Distress Syndrome (RDS) (hyaline membrane disease) in premature infants. SURVANTA significantly reduces the incidence of RDS, mortality due to RDS and air leak complications.

Prevention
In premature infants less than 1250 g birth weight or with evidence of surfactant deficiency, give SURVANTA as soon as possible, preferably within 15 minutes of birth.

Rescue
To treat infants with RDS confirmed by x-ray and requiring mechanical ventilation, give SURVANTA as soon as possible, preferably by 8 hours of age.

CONTRAINDICATIONS
None known.

WARNINGS
SURVANTA is intended for intratracheal use only.
SURVANTA CAN RAPIDLY AFFECT OXYGENATION AND LUNG COMPLIANCE. Therefore, its use should be restricted to a highly supervised clinical setting with immediate availability of clinicians experienced with intubation, ventilator management, and general care of premature infants. Infants receiving SURVANTA should be frequently monitored with arterial or transcutaneous measurement of systemic oxygen and carbon dioxide.
DURING THE DOSING PROCEDURE, TRANSIENT EPISODES OF BRADYCARDIA AND DECREASED OXYGEN SATURATION HAVE BEEN REPORTED. If these occur, stop the dosing procedure and initiate appropriate measures to alleviate the condition. After stabilization, resume the dosing procedure.

PRECAUTIONS
General
Rales and moist breath sounds can occur transiently after administration. Endotracheal suctioning or other remedial action is not necessary unless clear-cut signs of airway obstruction are present.
Increased probability of post-treatment nosocomial sepsis in SURVANTA-treated infants was observed in the controlled clinical trials (Table 3). The increased risk for sepsis among SURVANTA-treated infants was not associated with increased mortality among these infants. The causative organisms were similar in treated and control infants. There was no significant difference between groups in the rate of post-treatment infections other than sepsis.
Use of SURVANTA in infants less than 600 g birth weight or greater than 1750 g birth weight has not been evaluated in controlled trials. There is no controlled experience with use of SURVANTA in conjunction with experimental therapies for RDS (eg, high-frequency ventilation or extracorporeal membrane oxygenation).
No information is available on the effects of doses other than 100 mg phospholipids/kg, more than four doses, dosing more frequently than every 6 hours, or administration after 48 hours of age.

Carcinogenesis, Mutagenesis, Impairment of Fertility
Reproduction studies in animals have not been completed. Mutagenicity studies were negative. Carcinogenicity studies have not been performed with SURVANTA.

ADVERSE REACTIONS
The most commonly reported adverse experiences were associated with the dosing procedure. In the multiple-dose controlled clinical trials, transient bradycardia occurred with 11.9% of doses. Oxygen desaturation occurred with 9.8% of doses.
Other reactions during the dosing procedure occurred with fewer than 1% of doses and included endotracheal tube reflux, pallor, vasoconstriction, hypotension, endotracheal tube blockage, hypertension, hypocarbia, hypercarbia, and apnea. No deaths occurred during the dosing procedure, and all reactions resolved with symptomatic treatment.
The occurrence of concurrent illnesses common in premature infants was evaluated in the controlled trials. The rates in all controlled studies are in Table 3.

TABLE 3

	All Controlled Studies		
Concurrent Event	SURVANTA (%)	Control (%)	P Value[a]
Patent ductus arteriosus	46.9	47.1	0.814
Intracranial hemorrhage	48.1	15.2	0.749
Severe intracranial hemorrhage	24.1	27.2	0.630
Pulmonary air leaks	10.9	24.7	0.001
Pulmonary interstitial emphysema	22.2	39.4	0.001
Necrotizing enterocolitis	6.1	5.3	0.427
Apnea	66.4	59.6	0.283
Severe apnea	46.1	43.5	0.114
Post-treatment sepsis	20.7	16.1	0.019
Post-treatment infection	10.2	9.1	0.345
Pulmonary hemorrhage	7.2	5.3	0.166

[a] P value compares groups in controlled studies.

When all controlled studies were pooled, there was no difference in intracranial hemorrhage. However, in one of the single-dose rescue studies and one of the multiple-dose prevention studies, the rate of intracranial hemorrhage was significantly higher in SURVANTA patients than control patients (63.3% v 30.8%, P = 0.001; and 48.8% v 34.2%, P = 0.047, respectively). The rate in a Treatment IND involving approximately 4400 infants was lower than in the controlled trials.
In the controlled clinical trials, there was no effect of SURVANTA on results of common laboratory tests: white blood cell count and serum sodium, potassium, bilirubin, creatinine.
More than 3700 pretreatment and post-treatment serum samples were tested by Western Blot immunoassay for antibodies to surfactant-associated proteins SP-B and SP-C. No IgG or IgM antibodies were detected.
Several other complications are known to occur in premature infants. The following conditions were reported in the controlled clinical studies. The rates of the complications were not different in treated and control infants, and none of the complications were attributed to SURVANTA.
Respiratory: lung consolidation, blood from the endotracheal tube, deterioration after weaning, respiratory decompensation, subglottic stenosis, paralyzed diaphragm, respiratory failure.
Cardiovascular: hypotension, hypertension, tachycardia, ventricular tachycardia, aortic thrombosis, cardiac failure, cardiorespiratory arrest, increased apical pulse, persistent fetal circulation, air embolism, total anomalous pulmonary venous return.
Gastrointestinal: abdominal distention, hemorrhage, intestinal perforations, volvulus, bowel infarct, feeding intolerance, hepatic failure, stress ulcer.
Renal: renal failure, hematuria.
Hematologic: coagulopathy, thrombocytopenia, disseminated intravascular coagulation.
Central Nervous System: seizures.
Endocrine/Metabolic: adrenal hemorrhage, inappropriate ADH secretion, hyperphosphatemia.
Musculoskeletal: inguinal hernia.
Systemic: fever, deterioration.

Follow-Up Evaluations
To date, no long-term complications or sequelae of SURVANTA therapy have been found.

Single-Dose Studies
Six-month adjusted-age follow-up evaluations of 232 infants (115 treated) demonstrated no clinically important differences between treatment groups in pulmonary and neurologic sequelae, incidence or severity of retinopathy of prematurity, rehospitalizations, growth, or allergic manifestations.

Multiple-Dose Studies
Six-month adjusted age follow-up evaluations have not been completed. Preliminarily, in 605 (333 treated) of 916 surviving infants, there are trends for decreased cerebral palsy and need for supplemental oxygen in SURVANTA infants. Wheezing at the time of examination tended to be more frequent among SURVANTA infants, although there was no difference in bronchodilator therapy.
Twelve-month follow-up data from the multiple-dose studies have been completed in 326 (171 treated) of 909 surviving infants. To date no significant differences between treatments have been found, although there is a trend toward less wheezing in SURVANTA infants in contrast to the six month results.

OVERDOSAGE
Overdosage with SURVANTA has not been reported. Based on animal data, overdosage might result in acute airway obstruction. Treatment should be symptomatic and supportive.
Rales and moist breath sounds can transiently occur after SURVANTA is given, and do not indicate overdosage. Endotracheal suctioning or other remedial action is not required unless clear-cut signs of airway obstruction are present.

HOW SUPPLIED
SURVANTA (beractant) Intratracheal Suspension is supplied in single-use glass vials containing 8 mL of SURVANTA (NDC 0074-1040-08). Each milliliter contains 25 mg of phospholipids (200 mg phospholipids/ 8 mL) suspended in 0.9% sodium chloride solution. The color is off-white to light brown. Store unopened vials at refrigeration temperature (2-8°C). Protect from light. Store vials in carton until ready for use. Vials are for single use only. Upon opening, discard unused drug.

June, 1991

B401/2920

ROSS LABORATORIES

---

tracheal intubation for anesthesia (52), respiratory support (76), or CPR (23). INTERVENTIONS: After endotracheal intubation, tube position was verified, the detector was attached, and readings were obtained. MEASUREMENTS AND RESULTS: The detector correctly identified tube position (trachea, 124; esophagus, 4) in all 120 patients who were not in cardiac arrest ($p < 0.01$). In the cardiac arrest setting, all 6 esophageal intubations were correctly identified, but 2 of the 17 tracheal intubations were incorrectly interpreted as esophageal intubations ($p < 0.01$). CONCLUSION: The detector accurately identifies ETT position in children with spontaneous circulation who weigh more than 2 kg. During CPR, a positive test correctly indicates that the ETT is in the airway, but a negative result (suggesting esophageal placement) requires an alternate means of confirming ETT position.

Endotracheal Tube Whistle: An Adjunct to Blind Nasotracheal Intubation—S Krishel, K Jackimczyk, K Balazs. Ann Emerg Med 1992;21:33.

To perform blind nasotracheal intubation, the physician feels or listens for air movement through the endotracheal tube to facilitate the tube's passage into the trachea. The tube whistle is a device that attaches to the endotracheal tube adapter and

1992 Publication Awards

See Page 483 for more details.

produces whistle sounds of different pitches during inspiration and expiration, enhancing the detection of air movement and possibly allowing for easier intubation. This article describes the use of the whistle and presents information collected from a 9-mo prospective study of the endotracheal tube whistle.

Measuring the Impact of Standing Orders on Laboratory Utilization—J Studnicki, et al. Lab Med 1992;23:24.

A computerized information system for monitoring excessive laboratory tests was implemented. The system provides test frequency guidelines for both 1- and 7-day periods and accommodates both normal and abnormal values. Subsequently, a prohibition on standing orders allowed for an evaluation of its impact on test volumes and the extent of compliance with the guidelines. Before the prohibition, the overwhelming percentage of tests, which exceeded the frequency guidelines (ie, outliers), were within normal reference values and violations of the 7-day rules. During the prohibition on standing orders, test volumes decreased by 55%, test outliers decreased by 95%, and 7-day outliers were reduced from 90% to less than 50% of the total number of outliers. The analysis confirms that one of the most significant causes of excessive laboratory tests is the practice of daily testing in the absence of changes in test values.

Serum Magnesium Levels in Asthmatic Patients during Acute Exacerbations of Asthma—D Falkner, J Glauser, M Allen. Am J Emerg Med 1992;10:1.

The purpose of this study was to determine whether serum magnesium levels in asthmatic patients during acute exacerbations differ

from those of a control population. Twenty-three known asthmatics presenting to the emergency department in acute exacerbation (cases) and 15 nonasthmatic patients (controls) matched for age, sex, race, and socioeconomic status had serum magnesium assays drawn. Admission criteria were age 18 to 50 years with no history of alcoholism, heart disease, renal disease, or diuretic use. Patients giving a history of pregnancy were excluded. Serum magnesium levels were not significantly different in the two study populations, nor did they correlate with the severity of asthma (mean values: cases, 2.04 ± 0.159 versus controls, 2.03 ± 0.134 mg/dL; SD of the difference of the means = 0.048). An analysis for β-error demonstrated the true difference of the means to be < 0.1 (95% confidence) or < 0.13 (99% confidence). In conclusion, serum magnesium levels in asthmatics are not significantly different from those of a control nonasthmatic population. They are not clinically useful for predicting the severity of disease.

Effectiveness of Pressure Support Ventilation for Mechanical Ventilatory Support in Patients with Status Asthmaticus—H Tokioka, S Saito, T Takahashi, M Kinjo, S Saeki, F Kosaka, M Hirakawa. Acta Anaesthesiol Scand 1992;36:5.

We compared the effects of pressure support ventilation (PSV) with those of assist control ventilation (ACV) on breathing patterns and blood gas exchange in 6 patients with status asthmaticus. Both PSV and ACV delivered adequate minute ventilation (PSV: 7.5 ± 1.4 L/min/m², ACV: 7.3 ± 1.3 L/min/m²) to correct respiratory acidosis (pH = 7.33 ± 0.12 during both PSV and ACV) and prevent hypoxia. Peak airway pressure during PSV was significantly lower with the same tidal volume than that during ACV (PSV: 30 ± 10 cm H_2O, 2.9 ± 1.0 kPa; ACV: 50 ± 13 cm H_2O, 4.9 ± 1.3 kPa). The lower airway pressure during PSV was due to persistent inspiratory muscle activity. The oxygen cost of breathing estimated by oxygen consumption was equivalent in both modes. We conclude that PSV is effective in supplying tidal volumes adequate to improve hypercarbia at markedly lower airway pressures than ACV.

Variations in Asthma Hospitalizations and Death in New York City—W Carr, L Zeitel, K Weiss. Am J Public Health 1992;82:59.

BACKGROUND: Recent reports have identified New York City as having asthma mortality rates that are substantially higher than expected based on U.S. rates. This study investigates the problems of asthma morbidity and mortality in New York City. METHODS: Data on asthma hospitalizations (1982 to 1986) and deaths (1982 to 1987) among persons aged 0 to 34 years were studied. Descriptive and multivariate techniques were used to examine differences in rates among subgroups and across geographic areas. RESULTS: The average annual hospitalization rate was 39.2 per 10,000; the mortality rate was 1.2 per 100,000. Hospitalization and death rates among Blacks and Hispanics were 3 to 5.5 times those of Whites. Large geographic variations in hospitalizations and mortality occurred. Asthma hospitalization and mortality rates were highly correlated ($r = 0.67$), with the highest rates concentrated in the city's poorest neighborhoods. Household income, percentage of population Black and percentage of population Hispanic were significant predictors of area hospitalization rates (adjusted $R^2 = 0.75$). CONCLUSION: These findings provide a basis for focusing investigations of the causes of vari-

ations in asthma outcomes and targeting interventions to reduce the disproportionate morbidity and mortality borne by poor and minority populations.

Thoracic Complications of Extracorporeal Membrane Oxygenation: Findings on Chest Radiographs and Sonograms—GW Gross, J Cullen, MS Kornhauser, PJ Wolfson. Am J Radiol 1992;158: 353.

Neonates treated with extracorporeal membrane oxygenation (ECMO) for respiratory failure have a high frequency of complications related to systemic anticoagulation, ECMO, and other life-support lines and catheters, and the antecedent pulmonary disease. Many of these complications involve the thorax and can be defined on chest radiographs or thoracic sonograms. The purpose of this essay is to illustrate the findings of the various thoracic complications of ECMO on chest radiographs and sonograms. This study is based on a review of the medical records and findings on chest radiographs and sonograms of 150 neonates who were treated with ECMO at our institution.

Exposure to Environmental Tobacco Smoke in Naturalistic Settings—KM Emmons, DB Abrams, RJ Marshall, RA Etzel, TE Novotny, BH Marcus, ME Kane. Am J Public Health 1992;82:24.

BACKGROUND: Exposure to environmental tobacco smoke (ETS) has been identified as a risk factor for chronic disease among nonsmokers. Results of epidemiological surveys suggest that the majority of nonsmokers have regular ETS exposure. However, little is known about the topography of exposure. METHODS: An exposure diary was used by 186 nonsmokers to self-monitor

ETS exposure over a 7-day period. Subjects also completed a questionnaire that assessed their patterns of ETS exposure. RESULTS: The primary source of ETS exposure was the workplace, except when there was a smoker in the household, in which case the household was the primary source. The presence of a smoker in the household resulted in higher levels of exposure both at work and in other locations when compared with subjects without household exposure. Subjects' assessments of exposure on the questionnaire were consistently lower than their self-monitored levels. This finding suggests that general exposure ratings underestimate exposure. CONCLUSIONS: This study provides a new understanding of the patterns of ETS exposure and may help guide the development of policies and interventions designed to reduce ETS exposure.

Occupational Risks Associated with Cigarette Smoking: A Prospective Study—J Ryan, C Zwerling, EJ Orav. Am J Public Health 1992; 82:29.

BACKGROUND: Studies have indicated that cigarette smokers have more occupational accidents and injuries and use more sick time and health benefits than nonsmokers, thereby producing sizeable costs for employers. However, they usually have not controlled for other possible sources of these costs. We analyzed occupational costs associated with smoking while adjusting for a number of potential confounders. METHODS: We conducted a prospective, controlled study of the association between smoking and employment outcomes in 2,537 postal employees, adjusting for age, gender, race, drug use, job category, and exercise habits. RESULTS: For smokers, the relative risk for turnover was 1.01 (95% confidence interval [CI], 0.83-1.21);

for accidents 1.29 (CI, 1.07-1.55); for injuries 1.40 (CI, 1.11-1.77); for discipline 1.55 (CI, 1.19-2.02). Their mean absence rate was 5.43% compared with 4.06% for nonsmokers. CONCLUSIONS: Our study shows that cigarette smoking is associated with adverse employment outcomes after controlling for a number of possible confounders. This finding has implications for companies formulating smoking policies and considering the establishment of smoking cessation programs.

The Effect of State Cigarette Tax Increases on Cigarette Sales, 1955 to 1988—DE Peterson, SL Zeger, PL Remington, HA Anderson. Am J Public Health 1992;82:94.

We evaluated the effect of state cigarette tax increases on cigarette sales in the 50 states for the years 1955 to 1988. State cigarette tax increases were associated with an average decline in cigarette consumption of three cigarette packs per capita (about 2.4%). Larger tax increases were associated with larger declines in consumption. Raising state cigarette taxes appears to be an effective public health intervention that can reduce cigarette consumption and its associated health consequences.

Maternal Smoking and the Risk of Polyhydramnios—W Myhra, M Davis, BA Mueller, D Hickok. Am J Public Health 1992;82:176.

BACKGROUND: Washington State birth certificates were used to conduct a population-based case-control study to assess the possible association of maternal smoking with polyhydramnios. METHODS: All singleton births complicated by polyhydramnios (n = 557) were identified from the vital records for the years 1984 to 1987. For comparison, 1,671 records were randomly selected for the same years from singleton births

uncomplicated by polyhydramnios. RESULTS: Women who reportedly smoked prenatally were found to be at increased risk for polyhydramnios (relative risk [RR] = 1.7, 95% confidence interval [CI] = 1.5-2.1, adjusted for marital status, maternal age, and parity). When women with conditions known to be associated with polyhydramnios were excluded, the risk for those who smoked prenatally remained elevated (RR = 1.8, 95% CI = 1.1-2.3). CONCLUSION: Overdistention of the uterus with polyhydramnios may cause a variety of pregnancy complications. The observed association of smoking with polyhydramnios may be a further indication for public health interventions aimed at preventing smoking during pregnancy.

Cigarette, Alcohol, and Coffee Consumption and Prematurity—AD McDonald, BG Armstrong, M Sloan. Am J Public Health 1992; 82:87.

We analyzed data from a survey of occupational and other factors in pregnancy to assess the effects of cigarette, alcohol, and coffee consumption on pregnancy outcome. The risk of low birthweight for gestational age was found to increase substantially with smoking. Occasional consumers of alcohol had a slightly reduced risk relative to total abstainers. In more frequent drinkers, there was a small increase in risk. Risk increased slightly with coffee consumption.

Cigarette, Alcohol, and Coffee Consumption and Spontaneous Abortion—BG Armstong, AD McDonald, M Sloan. Am J Public Health 1992;82:85.

We analyzed data from a survey of occupational factors and pregnancy outcome to examine the effects of cigarette, alcohol, and coffee con-

sumption on pregnancy outcome. Clear and statistically significant associations were found between cigarette and alcohol consumption and spontaneous abortion. There was a weaker but statistically significant association with coffee consumption: If the associations were casual, 11% of the spontaneous abortions could be attributed to smoking, 5% to alcohol, and 2% to coffee.

Workplace Compliance with a No-Smoking Law: A Randomized Community Intervention Trial—NA Rigotti, D Bourne, A Rosen, JA Locke, TC Schelling. Am J Public Health 1992;82:229.

BACKGROUND: Compliance with state and local laws restricting smoking in public places and workplaces has not been systematically evaluated. METHODS: We assessed workplace compliance with a comprehensive no-smoking law adopted in Brookline MA and tested whether mailing information to businesses increased awareness of and compliance with the law. We conducted a random sample telephone survey of 299 businesses (87% response rate). Self-reported compliance was validated by direct observations. RESULTS: One year after its adoption, the law was popular with businesses. The prevalence of smoking restrictions, smoking policies, and no-smoking signs was 80%, 59%, and 40%, respectively. One third of businesses banned smoking. Full compliance with the law was low, however, because few businesses posted a copy of their smoking policy as required. The mailing increased employers' awareness of the law. Employers sent the mailing also reported better compliance, but this was not confirmed by direct observations. CONCLUSIONS: The law was popular and contributed to a high prevalence of workplace smoking restrictions. Different inter-

Need advanced ventilators but don't have the budget?

Take the strain out of dollar constraints with BEAR® Ventilator upgrades.

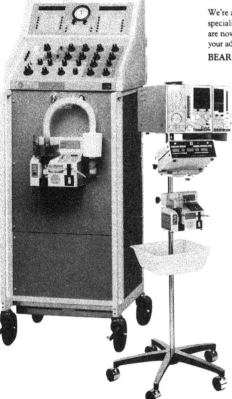

We're a group of authorized independent medical dealers specializing in BEAR Ventilators. Our service departments are now ready with two new *factory upgrades* priced to please your administration.

BEAR 1 to BEAR 3... and BEAR 2 to BEAR 3 Upgrades

- A genuine *factory* upgrade for a fraction of the new unit price!
- Includes advanced pressure support sytem, new one-year warranty.
- Proven performance now upgraded to help you manage still more patients.

BEAR CUB® to BEAR CUB 2 Upgrade

- A full *factory* upgrade at a surprisingly low price.
- Includes neonatal volume monitoring, SIMV, assist/control, and a new one-year warranty.
- Long the standard for infants now upgraded to a new standard!

Don't have a BEAR 1 or BEAR CUB Ventilator? We can help you, too!

Often we can obtain these popular ventilators as trade-ins and assemble the upgrades into complete, low cost packages for you. We can even schedule your local Bear representative to inservice your upgraded ventilators.

Act now!

This offer is good throughout the U.S. and Canada... but for a limited time only. Call **1-800-366-2327, ext. 4880** in the U.S. or **1-416-949-5444** in Canada for more information.

BEAR® and BEAR CUB® are registered trademarks of Bear Medical Systems, Inc.

Circle 129 on reader service card

pretations of the law of policymakers and businesses seemed to explain why formal compliance was low. The mailing increased awareness of, but not compliance with, the law.

Respiratory Muscle Training in Chronic Airflow Limitation: A Meta-Analysis—K Smith, D Cook, GH Guyatt, J Madhavan, AD Oxman. Am Rev Respir Dis 1992; 145:533.

SUMMARY: The purpose of this study was to determine the effect of respiratory muscle training on muscle strength and endurance, exercise capacity, and functional status in patients with chronic airflow limitation. Computerized bibliographic databases (MEDLINE AND SCI-SEARCH) were searched for published clinical trials, and an independent review of 73 articles by two of the investigators identified 17 relevant randomized trials for inclusion. Study quality was assessed and descriptive information concerning the study populations, interventions, and outcome measurements was extracted. We combined effect sizes across studies (the difference between treatment and control groups divided by the pooled standard deviation of the outcome measure). Across all studies, the effect sizes and associated p values were as follows: maximal inspiratory pressure 0.12, p = 0.38; maximal voluntary ventilation 0.43, p = 0.02; respiratory muscle endurance 0.21, p = 0.14; laboratory exercise capacity −0.01, p = 0.43; functional exercise capacity 0.20, p = 0.15; functional status 0.06, p = 0.72. Secondary analyses suggested that endurance and function may be improved if resistance training with control of breathing pattern is undertaken. Overall, there is little evidence of clinically important benefit of respiratory muscle training in patients with chronic airflow limitation. The possibility that benefit may result if resistance training is conducted in a fashion that ensures generation of adequate mouth pressures may be worthy of further study.

Childhood Asthma and Passive Smoking: Urinary Cotinine as a Biomarker of Exposure—R Ehrlich, M Kattan, J Godbold, DS Saltzberg, KT Grimm, PJ Landrigan, et al. Am Rev Respir Dis 1992;145:594.

SUMMARY: To assess the relationship between passive smoking and asthma, we investigated (1) whether passive smoking was more prevalent among asthmatic than control children and (2) whether exposure to tobacco smoke was higher in acute asthma than in nonacute asthma. Three groups were recruited into a case-control study: 72 acute asthmatic children from the emergency room (ER), 35 nonacute asthmatic children from the asthma clinic, and 121 control children from the ER. Both questionnaire and urinary continine/creatinine ratio (CCR) were used to assess passive smoking. Levels of CCR ≥ 30 ng/mg were used to identify children exposed at home. Mean CCR was also computed. Acute and nonacute asthmatic children had similar prevalences of passive smoking at home. Acute cases showed a higher mean CCR than nonacute cases, but this was not significant. In comparing all asthmatic to control children, smoking by the maternal caregiver was more prevalent among asthmatic children (odds ratio, OR = 2.0, 95% CI 1.1, 3.4). This was confirmed by CCR ≥ 30 ng/mg (OR = 1.9, 95% CI 1.04, 3.35) and by the difference in mean CCR (43.6 versus 25.8 ng/mg, p = 0.06). We conclude that smoking by the maternal caregiver is associated with clinically significant asthma in children. We could not show that it is a trigger of acute asthma attacks.

Comparison of Bronchial Reactivity and Peak Expiratory Flow Variability Measurements for Epidemiologic Studies—BG Higgins, JR Britton, S Chinn, S Cooper, PGJ Burney, AE Tattersfield. Am Rev Respir Dis 1992;145:588.

SUMMARY: Inclusion of a standardized measurement of airway function is important in epidemiologic studies of asthma to facilitate comparison between different studies. Bronchial reactivity is widely used in such studies, but measurement of peak expiratory flow (PEF) variability has a number of potential advantages. We compared PEF variability with methacholine challenge tests in a community population sample. Subjects selected at random (n = 95) and on the basis of having experienced wheeze in the last 12 months (n = 130) performed a challenge test with methacholine to a maximum dose of 12.25 μmol and made serial PEF recordings every 2 h for a week. PEF variability was expressed as mean daily maximum amplitude as a percentage of the mean (amplitude % mean). Increased bronchial reactivity and PEF variability were arbitrarily defined as values above the 10th or below the 90th percentiles in the random sample. A measurement of amplitude % mean was available from all 225 subjects, whereas only 115 (51%) had a measurable PD_{20} methacholine. PD_{20} measurements correlated weakly but significantly with amplitude % mean (r = −0.44, p < 0.001). Increased values of both bronchial reactivity and PEF variability were related to the presence of respiratory symptoms in the week before testing. Asthma was more strongly related to increased bronchial reactivity than to PEF variability. Both measurements showed a strong association with atopy and the intraclass correlation coefficients (ratio of between-subject to total variance) were similar for both. Thus,

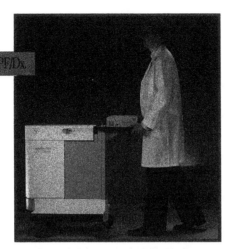

Introducing the PF/Dx.

Diagnose, treat, prevent heart and lung disease.
MedGraphics
Makes it easy.

Portable. Infection-control The new MedGraphics PF/Dx (pulmonary function diagnostic system) packs complete PF testing capabilities into a portable system. It's the only complete PFT system on the market to provide you with true infection control. Without chemicals, cleaning or filters. Freedom from cross-contamination is yours with the system's patented disposable pneumotach and snap-in-

snap-out breathing circuit. The system's pneumatic-glide arm, automatic calibration and easy-wheeling chassis let you test anyone, anywhere with incomparably accurate results.

Smart. Simple. MedGraphics friendly BREEZE software, with its colorful icons and prompts, guides you through tests on the PF/Dx. Operations are so automatic, you'll focus on the patient—not the system.

For a demonstration, more information or to find out about our other cost-effective heart and lung diagnostic products, call us today at:

MedGraphics®
Cardiorespiratory Diagnostic Systems

1-800-950-5597
or 1-612-484-4874

both PEF variability and bronchial reactivity are potentially useful markers for respiratory morbidity: Bronchial reactivity was a better marker for the diagnosis of asthma in the population, but PEF variability can supply a measurement in all subjects and may be preferable in longitudinal studies.

Effect of Uvulopalatopharyngoplasty on Upper Airway Collapsibility in Obstructive Sleep Apnea—AR Schwartz, N Schubert, W Rothman, F Godley, B Marsh, D Eisele, et al. Am Rev Respir Dis 1992;145:527.

SUMMARY: Previous investigators have demonstrated variable responses to uvulopalatopharyngoplasty (UPP) in patients with obstructive sleep apnea. We hypothesized that this variability is due to either (1) differences in baseline pharyngeal collapsibility preoperatively or (2) differences in magnitude of the decrease in pharyngeal collapsibility resulting from surgery. To determine the relationship between changes in collapsibility and the response to UPP surgery, we measured the upper airway critical pressure (P_{crit}) before and after UPP in 13 patients with obstructive sleep apnea. During non-REM sleep, maximal inspiratory airflow ($\dot{V}_{Imax}$) was quantitated by varying the level of nasal pressure (P_N) and P_{crit} was determined by the level of P_N below which $\dot{V}_{Imax}$ ceased. A positive response to UPP was defined by a $\geq 50\%$ fall in non-REM disordered breathing rate (DBR). In the entire group, UPP resulted in significant decreases in DBR from 71.1 ± 22.4 to 44.7 ± 38.4 episodes/h ($p = 0.025$) and in P_{crit} from 0.2 ± 2.4 to -3.1 ± 5.4 cm H_2O ($p = 0.016$). Moreover, the percent change in DBR was correlated significantly with the change in P_{crit} ($p = 0.001$). Subgroup analysis of responders and nonresponders demonstrated that significant differences in P_{crit} were confirmed to the responders. Specifically, responders demonstrated a significant fall in P_{crit} from -0.8 ± 3.0 to -7.3 ± 4.9 cm H_2O ($p = 0.01$), whereas no significant change in P_{crit} was detected in the nonresponders (1.1 ± 1.6 versus 0.6 ± 2.0 cm H_2O). No clinical, polysomnographic, or physiologic predictors of a favorable response were found preoperatively. We conclude that the response to UPP is determined by the magnitude of the fall in P_{crit} rather than by the initial preoperative level of P_{crit}. Several mechanisms to account for variability in the response of P_{crit} to surgery are suggested.

Oxygen Supplementation during Air Travel in Patients with Chronic Obstructive Lung Disease—BW Berg, TA Dillard, KR Rajagopal, WJ Mehm. Chest 1992; 101:638.

The objective of this study was to quantitate the effects of O_2 supplementation by nasal cannula (NC) and venturi mask (VM) on P_{aO_2} in patients with chronic obstructive cardiopulmonary disease (COPD) during acute hypobaric exposure, simulating a commercial jet aircraft cabin. We conducted a cross-over intervention trial in which subjects served as their own controls in an ambulatory outpatient pulmonary disease service of a tertiary care military medical center and a hypobaric research facility. The subjects were a volunteer sample of 18 men with stable severe COPD, not requiring long-term O_2 therapy, and uncomplicated by hypercapnia or cardiac disease. Mean age was 68 years, and mean FEV_1 was 0.97 L (31.3% predicted). We exposed patients to conditions equivalent to 8,000 feet in a hypobaric chamber. Radial artery catheters provided blood samples at ground level and 8,000 feet. O_2 was sequentially administerd at 8,000 feet by NC at 4 L/min and 24% or 28% VM. We describe changes in blood gas data from baseline values and between interventions. O_2 at 4 L/min NC flow at 8,000 feet caused P_{aO_2} to increase from 47.4 ± 6.3 torr to 82.3 ± 14 torr ($n = 18$), an increase of 34.9 ± 14.8 torr. Supplementation of O_2 by 24% VM caused P_{aO_2} at 8,000 feet to increase by 12.7 ± 3.8 torr. Twenty-eight percent VM caused P_{aO_2} at 8,000 feet to increase by 19.7 ± 8.2 torr. Changes in P_{aO_2} with 4 L/min NC were greater than those with either VM. The increase with 28% VM was greater than that caused by 24% VM ($p < 0.05$). Compared with ground level, 4 L/min NC increased mean P_{aO_2} by 9.9 ± 12.6 torr; 24% and 28% VM did not cause mean P_{aO_2} to increase above ground level values. We describe a range of capability of familiar O_2 therapy devices to increase P_{aO_2} to levels that will maintain tissue oxygenation of patients during acute altitude exposure.

A Model for Conversion from Small Volume Nebulizer to Metered Dose Inhaler Aerosol Therapy—MF Tenholder, MJ Bryson, WL Whitlock. Chest 1992;101: 634.

Rationing of medical services will be necessary if we do not develop a more rational and efficient health care system. Respiratory care services are receiving emphasis as we try to curtail spiraling health care costs. In analysis of our respiratory care services, we found that small volume nebulizer (SVN) therapy was still a major portion of our work load. We instituted a protocol to convert to metered dose inhaler (MDI) therapy. All hospitalized patients, excluding those admitted to the spinal cord unit and intensive care units, with a physician's order for aerosol delivery by SVN, were evaluated by respiratory care practitioners for con-

SURVIVING RDS
IS HARD ENOUGH...

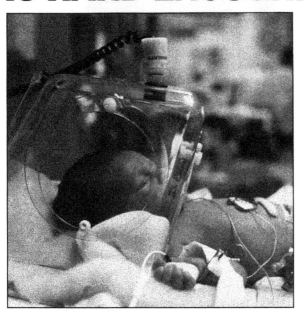

THE LAST THING
HE NEEDS IS IVH

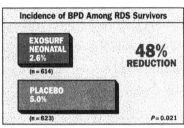
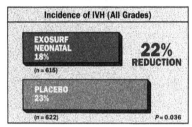

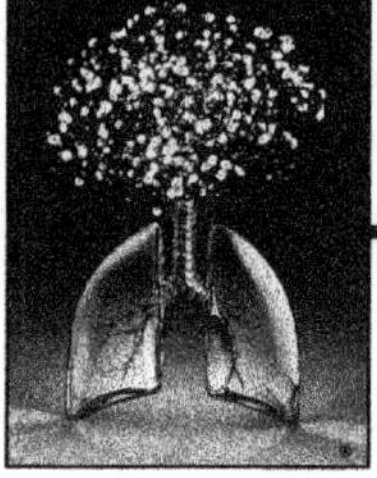

Exosurf® NEONATAL™
(Colfosceril Palmitate, Cetyl Alcohol, Tyloxapol) For Intratracheal Suspension/10-mL vial

INCREASES RDS SURVIVAL... REDUCES RISKS*

*Increased pulmonary hemorrhage was noted in one trial of infants 500-699 g[7]; increased apnea has been noted in some trials.[1,2,8]

PLEASE CONSULT FULL PRODUCT INFORMATION BEFORE PRESCRIBING

INDICATIONS AND USAGE: Exosurf Neonatal is indicated for: 1. **Prophylactic** treatment of infants with birth weights of less than 1350 grams who are at risk of developing RDS (see PRECAUTIONS). 2. **Prophylactic** treatment of infants with birth weights greater than 1350 grams who have evidence of pulmonary immaturity, and 3. **Rescue** treatment of infants who have developed RDS.

CONTRAINDICATIONS: There are no known contraindications to treatment with Exosurf Neonatal.

WARNINGS: **Intratracheal Administration Only:** Exosurf Neonatal should be administered only by instillation into the trachea (see DOSAGE AND ADMINISTRATION). **General:** The use of Exosurf Neonatal requires expert clinical care by experienced neonatologists and other clinicians who are accomplished at neonatal intubation and ventilatory management. Adequate personnel, facilities, equipment, and medications are required to optimize perinatal outcome in premature infants. Vigilant clinical attention should be given to all infants prior to, during, and after administration of Exosurf Neonatal. **Acute Effects:** Exosurf Neonatal can rapidly affect oxygenation and lung compliance. **Lung Compliance:** If chest expansion improves substantially after dosing, peak ventilator inspiratory pressures should be reduced immediately, without waiting for confirmation of respiratory improvement by blood gas assessment. Failure to reduce inspiratory ventilator pressures rapidly in such instances can result in lung overdistention and fatal pulmonary air leak. **Hyperoxia:** If the infant becomes pink and transcutaneous oxygen saturation is in excess of 95%, FiO_2 should be reduced in small but repeated steps (until saturation is 90 to 95%) without waiting for confirmation of elevated arterial pO_2 by blood gas assessment. Failure to reduce FiO_2 in such instances can result in hyperoxia. **Hypocarbia:** If arterial or transcutaneous CO_2 measurements are <30 torr, the ventilator rate should be reduced at once. Failure to reduce ventilator rates in such instances can result in marked hypocarbia, which is known to reduce brain blood flow. **Pulmonary Hemorrhage:** In the single study conducted in infants weighing <700 grams at birth, the incidence of pulmonary hemorrhage (10% vs 2% in the placebo group) was significantly increased in the Exosurf Neonatal group. None of the five studies involving infants with birth weights >700 grams showed a significant increase in pulmonary hemorrhage in the Exosurf Neonatal group. In a cross-study analysis of these five studies, fatal pulmonary hemorrhage occurred in three infants; two in the Exosurf Neonatal group and one in the placebo group. Mortality from all causes among infants who developed pulmonary hemorrhage was 43% in the placebo group and 37% in the Exosurf Neonatal group. Pulmonary hemorrhage in both Exosurf Neonatal and placebo infants was more frequent in infants who were younger, smaller, male, or who had a patent ductus arteriosus. Pulmonary hemorrhage typically occurred in the first 2 days of life in both treatment groups. **Mucous Plugs:** Infants whose ventilation becomes markedly impaired during or shortly after dosing may have mucous plugging of the endotracheal tube, particularly if pulmonary secretions were prominent prior to drug administration. Suctioning of all infants prior to dosing may lessen the chance of mucous plugs obstructing the endotracheal tube. If endotracheal tube obstruction from such plugs is suspected, and suctioning is unsuccessful in removing the obstruction, the blocked endotracheal tube should be replaced immediately.

PRECAUTIONS: **General:** In the controlled clinical studies, infants known prenatally or postnatally to have major congenital anomalies, or who were suspected of having congenital infection, were excluded from entry. However, these disorders cannot be recognized early in life in all cases, and a few infants with these conditions were entered. The benefits of Exosurf Neonatal in the affected infants who received drug appeared to be similar to the benefits observed in infants without anomalies or occult infection. **Prophylactic Treatment—Infants <700 Grams:** In infants weighing 500 to 700 grams, a single prophylactic dose of Exosurf Neonatal significantly: improved FiO_2 and ventilator settings, reduced pneumothorax, and reduced death from RDS, but increased pulmonary hemorrhage (see WARNINGS). Overall mortality did not differ significantly between the placebo and Exosurf Neonatal groups. Data on multiple doses in infants in this weight class are not yet available. **Rescue Treatment—Number of Doses:** A small number of infants with RDS have received more than two doses of Exosurf Neonatal as rescue treatment. Definitive data on the safety and efficacy of these additional doses are not available. **Carcinogenesis, Mutagenesis, Impairment of Fertility:** Exosurf Neonatal at concentrations up to 10,000 µg/plate was not mutagenic in the Ames Salmonella assay. Long-term studies have not been performed in animals to evaluate the carcinogenic potential of Exosurf Neonatal. The effects of Exosurf Neonatal on fertility have not been studied.

ADVERSE REACTIONS:
General: Premature birth is associated with a high incidence of morbidity and mortality. Despite significant reductions in overall mortality associated with Exosurf Neonatal, some infants who received Exosurf Neonatal developed severe complications and either survived with permanent handicaps or died. In controlled clinical studies evaluating the safety and efficacy of Exosurf Neonatal, numerous safety assessments were made. In infants receiving Exosurf Neonatal, pulmonary hemorrhage, apnea and use of methylxanthines were increased. A number of other adverse events were significantly reduced in the Exosurf Neonatal group, particularly various forms of pulmonary air leak and use of pancuronium. ***Reflux:*** Reflux of Exosurf Neonatal into the endotracheal tube during dosing has been observed and may be associated with rapid drug administration. If reflux occurs, drug administration should be halted and, if necessary, peak inspiratory pressure on the ventilator should be increased by 4 to 5 cm H_2O until the endotracheal tube clears. ***>20% Drop in Transcutaneous Oxygen Saturation:*** If transcutaneous oxygen saturation declines during dosing, drug administration should be halted and, if necessary, peak inspiratory pressure on the ventilator should be increased by 4 to 5 cm H_2O for 1 to 2 minutes. In addition, increases of FiO_2 may be required for 1 to 2 minutes.

DOSAGE AND ADMINISTRATION: **Preparation of Suspension:** Exosurf Neonatal is best reconstituted immediately before use because it does not contain antibacterial preservatives. However, the reconstituted suspension is chemically and physically stable when stored at 2° to 30°C (36° to 86°F) for up to 12 hours following reconstitution. Solutions containing buffers or preservatives should not be used for reconstitution. **Do Not Use Bacteriostatic Water for Injection, USP.** Each vial of Exosurf Neonatal should be reconstituted only with **8 mL** of the accompanying diluent (preservative-free Sterile Water for Injection). **Dosage: Accurate determination of weight at birth is the key to accurate dosing.** *Prophylactic Treatment:* The first dose of Exosurf Neonatal should be administered as a single 5 mL/kg dose as soon as possible after birth. Second and third doses should be administered approximately 12 and 24 hours later to all infants who remain on mechanical ventilation at those times. ***Rescue Treatment:*** Exosurf Neonatal should be administered in two 5 mL/kg doses. The initial dose should be administered as soon as possible after the diagnosis of RDS is confirmed. The second dose should be administered approximately 12 hours following the first dose, provided the infant remains on mechanical ventilation. **Use of Special Endotracheal Tube Adapter:** With each vial of Exosurf Neonatal for Intratracheal Suspension, five different sized endotracheal tube adapters each with a special right angle Luer®-lock sideport are supplied. The adapters are clean but not sterile. **Administration:** The infant should be suctioned prior to administration of Exosurf Neonatal. Exosurf Neonatal suspension is administered via the sideport on the special endotracheal tube adapter WITHOUT INTERRUPTING MECHANICAL VENTILATION. Each Exosurf Neonatal dose is administered in two 2.5 mL/kg half-doses. Each half-dose is instilled slowly over 1 to 2 minutes (30 to 50 mechanical breaths) in small bursts timed with inspiration. After the first 2.5 mL/kg half-dose is administered in the midline position, the infant's head and torso are turned 45° to the **right** for 30 seconds while mechanical ventilation is continued. After the infant is returned to the midline position, the second 2.5 mL/kg half-dose is given in an identical fashion over another 1 to 2 minutes. The infant's head and torso are then turned 45° to the **left** for 30 seconds while mechanical ventilation is continued, and the infant is then turned back to the midline position. These maneuvers allow gravity to assist in the distribution of Exosurf Neonatal in the lungs. During dosing, heart rate, color, chest expansion, facial expressions, the oximeter, and the endotracheal tube patency and position should be monitored. **Suctioning should not be performed for two hours after Exosurf Neonatal is administered, except when dictated** by clinical **necessity.**

HOW SUPPLIED: Exosurf Neonatal for Intratracheal Suspension is supplied in a carton containing one 10 mL vial of Exosurf Neonatal for Intratracheal Suspension, one 10 mL vial of Sterile Water for Injection, and five endotracheal tube adapters (2.5, 3.0, 3.5, 4.0, and 4.5 mm I.D.). (NDC 0081-0207-01). Store Exosurf Neonatal for Intratracheal Suspension at 15° to 30°C (59° to 86°F) in a dry place.

EDUCATIONAL MATERIAL: A videotape on dosing is available from your Burroughs Wellcome Co. representative. This videotape demonstrates techniques for safe administration of Exosurf Neonatal and should be viewed by health care professionals who will administer the drug.

Licensed under U.S. Patent Nos. 4312860 and 4826821 500009

References: 1. Long W, Thompson T, Sundell H, et al. Effects of two rescue doses of a synthetic surfactant on mortality rate and survival without bronchopulmonary dysplasia in 700- to 1350-gram infants with respiratory distress syndrome. *J Pediatr.* 1991;118:595-605. 2. Long W, Corbet A, Cotton R, et al. A controlled trial of synthetic surfactant in infants weighing 1250 g or more with respiratory distress syndrome. *N Engl J Med.* 1991;325:1696-1703. 3. Speer CP, Robertson B, Curstedt T, et al. Randomized European multicenter trial of surfactant replacement therapy for severe neonatal respiratory distress syndrome: single versus multiple doses of Curosurf. *Pediatrics.* 1992;89:13-20. 4. Horbar JD, Soll RF, Schachinger H, et al. A European multicenter randomized controlled trial of single dose surfactant therapy for idiopathic respiratory distress syndrome. *Eur J Pediatr.* 1990;149:416-423. 5. Cowan F, Whitelaw A, Wertheim D, Silverman M. Cerebral blood flow velocity changes after rapid administration of surfactant. *Arch Dis Child.* 1991;66:1105-1109. 6. Russell L, White A, Andrews E, et al. Observational study of synthetic surfactant in 11,455 infants. Presented at the 1992 Meeting of the American Pediatric Society/Society for Pediatric Research; May 4-7, 1992; Baltimore, MD. 7. Stevenson D, Walther F, Long W, et al. Controlled trial of a single dose of synthetic surfactant at birth in premature infants weighing 500 to 699 grams. *J Pediatr.* 1992;120:S3-S12. 8. Corbet A, Bucciarelli R, Goldman S, et al. Decreased mortality rate among small premature infants treated at birth with a single dose of synthetic surfactant: a multicenter controlled trial. *J Pediatr.* 1991;118 277-284

Burroughs Wellcome Co.
Wellcome Research Triangle Park, NC 27709

version to MDI therapy. A simple protocol for the therapist to use in this conversion was developed. All patients converted to MDI were trained in appropriate MDI use by the therapist. A 3-day follow-up of each patient's compliance with proper MDI therapy was initiated. Even with a 72-h allowance for initial SVN treatment, we realized a 9,350 procedure reduction from deleted treatments and an additional 7,650 conversions to MDI. Less than 2% of our patients failed to make a completely successful conversion to MDI. Those patients who successfully converted to MDI resulted in reduced hospital costs of $43,758 based on excess medication, supplies, and labor costs associated with SVN treatments. We also saved 5,000 h of technician time that was used to further instruct patients in appropriate MDI therapy. Aerosol therapy by MDI is cost-effective therapy. The institution of guidelines for MDI conversion has reduced fear of failure for both clinicians and patients and illustrates the importance of patient education by qualified respiratory therapists.

The Fatality-Prone Asthmatic Patient: Follow-Up Study after Near-Fatal Attacks—NA Molfino, LJ Nannini, AS Rebuck, AS Slutsky. Chest 1992;101:621.

We studied 12 fatality-prone patients for 18 months after they had been discharged from the hospital following life-threatening exacerbations of asthma (mean Pa_{CO_2} on admission, 97 torr). Our objectives were (1) to evaluate the natural history of their disease during ambulatory care and (2) to investigate whether close follow-up might help to avert further near-fatal events. Only 7 of the 12 patients consented to be enrolled in the study, which included monthly scheduled visits to the hospital and monthly telephone calls to record emergency room visits and changes in therapy. By the conclusion of the 18-month follow-up period, two of the noncompliant patients had died during asthmatic attacks. By contrast, all of the 7 who had agreed to participate survived; 1 required intubation and mechanical ventilation, and the other 6 required occasional unscheduled emergency room visits because of acute exacerbations. Specific precipitants could not be determined, and the most common cause of the acute episodes was likely inadequate steroid therapy. The results suggest that compliance with adequate antiasthmatic therapy and close follow-up may be important in the prevention of near-fatal events.

Reversibility of Airways Injury over a 12-Month Period following Smoking Cessation—GE Swan, JE Hodgkin, T Roby, C Mittman, N Jacobo, J Peters. Chest 1992;101:607.

In this investigation, we examined changes in exfoliated tracheobronchial cells in sputum in 46 individuals (mean age = 49.2 years; mean pack-years = 48.7) who discontinued smoking and 37 individuals (mean age = 54.9 years; mean pack-years = 65.2) who continued to smoke over a 12-month period after participation in the St Helena Hospital and Health Center 1-week residential smoking cessation program. Before the beginning of the smoking cessation program, those who went on to quit were not different from those who did not quit with respect to baseline cytomorphology ratings. In those individuals with a minimum of three follow-up tests, results indicated significant reductions from precessation levels in macrophages, pigmented macrophages, and neutrophils after adjustment for differences in age, pack-years, and pulmonary function (FEV_1/FVC). Over the course of follow-up, quitters, in comparison with nonquitters, also had significantly lower mean levels of columnar cells, mucus, mucous spirals, and metaplasia. These results indicate a consistent effect of smoking cessation on cytomorphology and demonstrate that on cessation, some of the measured elements promptly return toward a more normal pattern.

Effects of Inhaled Oxygen (Up to 40%) on Periodic Breathing and Apnea in Preterm Infants—Z Weintraub, R Alvaro, K Kwiatkowski, D Cates, H Rigatto. J Appl Physiol 1992;72(1):116.

To discover whether increases in inhaled O_2 fraction (F_{IO_2}, up to 40%) decrease apnea via an increase in minute ventilation ($\dot{V}_E$) or a change in respiratory pattern, 15 preterm infants (birthweight $1,300 \pm 354$ g, gestational age 29 ± 2 wk, postnatal age 20 ± 9 days) breathed 21, 25, 30, 35, and 40% O_2 for 10 min in quiet sleep. A nosepiece and a flow-through system were used to measure ventilation. Alveolar P_{CO_2}, transcutaneous P_{O_2}, and sleep states were also assessed. All infants had periodic breathing with apneas ≥ 3 s. With an increase in F_{IO_2}, breathing became more regular and apneas decreased ($p < 0.001$). This regularization in breathing was not associated with significant changes in $\dot{V}_E$. However, the variability of $\dot{V}_E$, tidal volume, and expiratory and inspiratory times decreased significantly. The results indicate that the more regular breathing observed with small increases in F_{IO_2} was not associated with significant changes in ventilation. The findings suggest that the increased oxygenation decreases apnea and periodicity in preterm infants, not via an increase in ventilation, but through a decrease in breath-to-breath variability of $\dot{V}_E$.

Editorials

Chest Physical Therapy:
Time for a Redefinition and a Renaming

In April 1991, RESPIRATORY CARE published an extensive review of chest physical therapy (CPT) by Eid and colleagues.[1] These authors appear to be in general agreement with many others[2-8] that CPT has a very short list of indications and often can be harmful when used in other circumstances. The string of negative editorials, reviews, and commentaries seems to have originated with Murray's "ketchup-bottle" editorial in 1979.[9] The first report of an effective program to assure that CPT treatments (and other forms of respiratory therapy) conformed to rational guidelines appeared in the pages of this Journal nearly a decade ago.[10] Surely sufficient time has elapsed for the message to sink in—CPT is not a panacea. By now, the *routine* use of CPT in patients with uncomplicated pneumonia, postoperative patients, and patients with asthma and COPD—and on and on—should only be a distant memory, lodged in our brains somewhere between IPPB and bland aerosol treatments via ultrasonic nebulizer.

Sadly, this appears not to be the case. In my institution, for example, the use of CPT has increased 260% over the last decade. I suspect we are not alone. Recently, I conducted a survey of 56 children's hospitals and 50 general hospitals with large pediatric departments to quantify CPT utilization patterns in pediatrics.[11] Suspecting as always that "the grass is greener on the other side," I expected the survey to reveal that my hospital performs more treatments per year than any other comparable institution in the country. I was surprised to learn that the utilization rate in our hospital was not too far off the national median of 136 treatments per bed per year; and the survey revealed some other surprising facts as well. Nearly 50% of hospitals have no automatic stop policy, and a similar number report having no mech-

anisms, such as periodic patient evaluations, to limit the number of unnecessary treatments. And this is an era of cost-containment!!?? Not so surprising was the finding that hospitals with automatic stop orders have significantly fewer treatments per bed per year (132) than those with no policy (261) (p < 0.05, Wilcoxon rank sum test).

Much CPT is given to patients who will not benefit from it. The Eid et al review[1] and other publications[12-14] clearly agree that CPT is of no value in pneumonia; yet, pneumonia tops the list of my respondents' "very common" indications. Furthermore, the survey shows that many hospitals use CPT frequently for pediatric postoperative patients, and for those with asthma and bronchiolitis, conditions where evidence of benefit is likewise lacking.[15,16]

Nearly two decades ago, similar figures and arguments were cited to describe the misuse and overuse of IPPB therapy. Longtime readers of RESPIRATORY CARE will recall issue after issue featuring opinions and viewpoints on "the great debate." In most hospitals, people seemed to listen, and IPPB usage has fallen dramatically. Why has the struggle to reduce unnecessary CPT not met with similar success?

I believe the reason is that we had effective alternatives to offer in place of IPPB. Incentive spirometry was available for postoperative patients; simple nebulizers were available for those with reactive airway diseases; and CPT was available for those with secretion mobilization problems. But now we know that CPT has little to offer most patients with acute or chronic pulmonary diseases. What can we offer in its place to physicians who treat these patients?

Before answering this question, we need to know why physicians order CPT. What are they trying to accomplish? I believe most physicians are more concerned with results than processes. When ordering CPT, they are not so much ordering a fixed sequence of positioning, percussion, and vibration as saying "do what you can to mobilize and remove secretions." Then why do so few of us feel comfortable simply spending a few minutes encouraging deep breathing and coughing when deep breathing and coughing may be all that is needed to achieve the desired results in many cases, and are consistent with *some* definitions[6] of "chest physical therapy"? Most respiratory care departments began CPT programs in the late 1960s or early 1970s, often using techniques developed at the Brompton Hospital during that era.[17] Although knowledge of what works and what doesn't (ie, what is and what isn't chest physical therapy) has evolved, for most of us, our CPT *practices* are frozen in time, unfortunately. We have chosen to define CPT in a way that limits the practitioner's ability to apply *only* those techniques necessary to achieve the desired results.

It is interesting to note, judging from selected items appearing in the medical literature,[18-20] that the virtual inventors of modern CPT have a much more flexible and dynamic approach to what is and is not incorporated into a CPT treatment. Perhaps many respiratory care practitioners in the U.S. feel CPT is imported, both literally and figuratively, from another discipline (physical therapy) on another continent. Indeed, physical therapists have contributed far more to the scientific literature on CPT than have respiratory care practitioners. And, with few exceptions, I believe that the literature of interest about CPT has come from Europe, Australia, or Canada. Nevertheless, it is perfectly appropriate for us as respiratory care practitioners to claim CPT as our own. This does not mean fighting political battles with our sister professions over control of this therapy, but, rather, accepting the responsibility to base all of our practice on firm scientific principles, regardless of the origins of a particular technique.

Rather than offer our patients and the physicians who treat them a new 'process,' some new therapy as an alternative to CPT, I propose that we redefine and rename CPT in such a way that it frees us to focus on ends, not means. Several years ago, we began referring to chest physical therapy as bron-

chial drainage, in my hospital. This term emphasizes the goals of CPT, rather than the process. If we were to adjust our thinking accordingly, focusing on the goal implied in the term bronchial drainage would allow individualized assessment and application of those techniques that achieve our goal, yet minimize complications, cost, time, and discomfort.

Most departments I surveyed (including my own) view CPT as a relatively fixed combination of techniques applied in a consistent fashion for a predetermined length of time to all patients, regardless of need or response. For example, half the respondents indicated that, unless ordered otherwise, CPT was applied to all lung fields, regardless of the particular disorder being treated. Few of us seem to realize that we, collectively and as individual departments, have the power to define exactly what is and is not CPT. CPT needs to be continually redefined so that clinicians are free to incorporate the ever-evolving body of knowledge into their practice, and—just as importantly—to drop outdated or unnecessary procedures and techniques. It is the therapist, not the ordering physician, who must choose the appropriate techniques to apply.

The AARC Clinical Practice Guideline for Postural Drainage Therapy,[21] published in December 1991, takes a significant step toward giving therapists that freedom. These guidelines can be taken as a signal that a national consensus exists that our definition of CPT (aka bronchial drainage, postural drainage) must be flexible, dynamic, and patient-disease specific. Department managers and medical directors should now take the next step and discard policies and procedures that do not allow the bedside therapist the freedom and flexibility to employ only those techniques needed to attain the therapeutic objective. For example, department procedures should be revised so that, when appropriate, directed coughing or endotracheal suction alone can be applied if they meet the therapeutic objective of bronchial drainage. This approach to the delivery of care (therapist-driven protocols) was discussed extensively at our recent Annual Meeting, and has been described as well in the *AARC Times*.[22]

Redefining CPT is not a substitute for efforts to ensure that all ordering practices and therapies have a scientific basis, but I believe that redefining and renaming CPT is well within the scope of responsibilities of the respiratory care department and its medical director, and is long overdue.

Such a move could be a first step toward freeing bedside practitioners to select, apply, and modify therapy based on patient response.

Robert M Lewis BA RRT
Clinical Coordinator
Respiratory Care
The Children's Memorial Hospital
Chicago, Illinois

Reprints: Robert M Lewis BA RRT, Respiratory Care, Box 58, The Children's Memorial Hospital, 2300 Children's Pl, Chicago IL 60614.

REFERENCES

1. Eid N, Buchheit J, Neuling M, Phelps H. Chest physiotherapy in review. Respir Care 1991;36:270-282.
2. Andersen JB, Falk M. Chest physiotherapy in the pediatric age group. Respir Care 1991;36:546-554.
3. Kirilloff LH, Owens GR, Rogers RM, Mazzocco MC. Does chest physical therapy work? Chest 1985;88:436-444.
4. Pavia D. The role of chest physiotherapy in mucus hypersecretion. Lung 1990;168(Suppl):614-621.
5. Selsby DS. Chest physiotherapy may be harmful in some patients. Br Med J 1989;298:541-542.
6. Selsby D, Jones JG. Some physiological and clinical aspects of chest physiotherapy. Br J Anaesth 1990;64:621-631.
7. Stiller KR, McEvoy RD. Chest physiotherapy for the medical patient—are current practices effective? Aust NZ J Med 1990;20:183-187.
8. Sutton PP, Pavia D, Bateman JRM, Clarke SW. Chest physiotherapy: a review. Eur J Respir Dis 1982;63:188-201.
9. Murray JF. The ketchup-bottle method (editorial). N Engl J Med 1979;300:1155-1157.
10. Walton JR, Shapiro BA, Harrison CH. Review of a bronchial hygiene evaluation program Respir Care 1983;28:174-179.
11. Lewis R. Chest physical therapy in pediatrics: a national survey (abstract). Respir Care 1991;36:1307-1308.
12. Stapleton T. Chest physiotherapy in primary pneumonia (letter). Br Med J 1985;291:143.
13. Britton S, Bejstedt M, Vedin L. Chest physiotherapy in primary pneumonia. Br Med J 1985;290:1703-1704.
14. Graham WGB, Bradley DA. Efficacy of chest physiotherapy and intermittent positive-pressure breathing in the resolution of pneumonia. N Engl J Med 1978; 299: 624-627.
15. Asher MI, Douglas C, Airy M, Andrews D, Threnholme A. Effects of chest physical therapy on lung function in children recovering from acute severe asthma. Pediatr Pulmonol 1990;9:146-151.
16. Webb MSC, Martin J, Cartlidge P, Ng Y, Wright N. Chest physiotherapy in acute bronchiolitis. Arch Dis Child 1985;60:1078-1079.
17. Gaskell DV, Webber BA. The Brompton hospital guide to chest physiotherapy, 2nd ed. Oxford: Blackwell Scientific Publications, 1973.
18. Sutton PP, Parker RA, Webber BA, Newman SP, Garland N, Lopez-Vidriero MT, et al. Assessment of the forced expiratory technique, postural drainage and directed coughing in chest physiotherapy. Eur J Respir Dis 1983;64:62-68.
19. Sutton PP, Lopez-Vidriero MT, Pavia D, Newman SP, Clay MM, Webber B, et al. Assessment of percussion, vibratory-shaking and breathing excercises in chest physiotherapy. Eur J Respir Dis 1985;66:147-152.
20. Webber BA, Pryor JA. Respiratory physiotherapy for cystic fibrosis (letter). J Pediatr 1989;115:167-168.
21. Bronchial Hygiene Guidelines Committee, American Association for Respiratory Care. AARC clinical practice guideline: postural drainage therapy. Respir Care 1991;36:1418-1426.
22. Tietsort J. The respiratory care protocol: a management tool for the 1990's. AARCTimes 1991;15(5):54-58.

A New Journal Feature—Kittredge's Corner: Technical Aspects of Respiratory Care

Respiratory care practitioners play an important and unique role in the health care system. No other profession combines the elements of direct hands-on patient care with the use of sophisticated technical equipment as we do.

However, to fulfill this role, we must keep abreast of advances in both clinical medicine and in technology, and its appropriate application. This is not an easy task. The speed at which technologic changes are made and the plethora of new equipment introduced to the marketplace are astounding.

RESPIRATORY CARE is (as it should be) the single best reference we have to keep us up to date on these changes. Yet, it has been our observation, and personal experience, that none of us is as familiar with the operation of equipment as we could be. The quirks and intricacies of modern-day ventilators are an example. Two or more manufacturers may use the same term for ventilator features that are quite different. To fully understand and appreciate this, we have to spend time reading the operators' manuals, which average about 100 pages per ventilator. Time constraints limit the number of manuals and product updates that we can read and re-read. We use "we" and "us" intentionally, not excluding ourselves from this problem. And, we hasten to add that pointing out the problem is easy; defining a solution is the difficult part.

As a part of the solution, we introduce a new feature to the Journal. Kittredge's Corner will be devoted to brief, to-the-point summaries of facets of the operation of respiratory care equipment. Each Corner will review the literature on the topic in question (eg, preoxygenation for suctioning the ventilator patient) not to exhaustion but to set the scene for why and how this is important. A description of how specific pieces of equipment handle the same function will follow (eg, What happens when you depress the 100% suction button on Ventilator X?). Descriptions will be in enough detail to allow the clinician to scrutinize the functions. These will not be evaluations, but simply descriptions of how specific pieces of equipment accomplish a certain function. We have enlisted the manufacturers as resources for information not readily available in the manuals. We also hope that interaction with the manufacturers will minimize misunderstandings, prevent mistakes, and enhance the relationship between manufacturers and clinicians. At the end of each Corner, we will exercise editorial privilege in commenting on the performance of equipment, suggesting improvements, and pointing out topics for clinical research.

As editors of the Corner, we have pledged to write a minimum of four Corners each year. However, we encourage reader-clinicians to become involved and to submit their own Kittredge's Corners. If you would like to prepare a Corner, please write. We will be happy to assist you with the format and help you contact the manufacturers' representatives.

We have chosen the title "Kittredge's Corner" to honor Phil Kittredge RRT. During his 21-year association with the Journal as Editor and Adjunct Editor, Phil's contributions have been countless. In fact, the Journal survived in the lean years by his wit and ingenuity. His influence on the writings of the most published authors in this Journal may not be obvious, but certainly many of us are indebted to Phil for his stern editorial hand and gentle criticisms. Aside from his excellent performance on the job, Phil is a kind-spirited, humorous, learned man of substance who we are honored to call friend. Many of us continue to receive unsolicited notes, clippings, and cartoons from Phil, which brighten our days and enlighten our minds. We hope to create a feature that will live up to its namesake.

To paraphrase the words of a wise man (Albert Einstein)—everything should be explained as simply as necessary, but not one bit simpler.

Richard D Branson RRT
Department of Surgery

Robert S Campbell RRT
Department of Respiratory Care

University of Cincinnati Medical Center
Cincinnati, Ohio

Original Contributions

Effect of a New Nebulizer Position on Aerosol Delivery during Mechanical Ventilation: A Bench Study

William W Quinn RPFT RRT

BACKGROUND: The efficacy of placing nebulizers at the Y-piece vs at the manifold during mechanical ventilation (MV) has been reported, as have the effects of intermittent vs continuous nebulization. I studied the effects of a new nebulizer position, at the ventilator end of the circuit, by nebulizing food coloring at a target and using a colorimetry scale to quantitate aerosol delivery under various conditions. MATERIALS & METHODS: To create the visual colorimetry scale, I colored white bacteria filters yellow with nebulized food coloring, then exposed 30 of them for graded periods of time to nebulized blue food coloring, creating a colorimetry scale ranging from light yellow-green (Filter #1, exposed 5 s) to dark blue-green (Filter #30, exposed 150 s). *Test Setup:* A nebulizer was placed variously at the Y-piece, manifold, and ventilator positions in a P-B 7200 ventilator circuit. The distal end of the circuit was attached to an endotracheal tube that had a plain yellow target filter attached to its 'tracheal' end. *Testing:* Blue food coloring was nebulized during simulated MV, and the aerosol impacted on and colored the target filter. Continuous and intermittent nebulization and the different nebulizer positions were studied in seven combinations of position and mode. A 3-person jury then assigned, by consensus, a colorimetry-scale value to each target filter. The resulting number score for each test condition was then compared to scores for the other test conditions, yielding data showing which nebulizer conditions allowed more or less coloring (representing medication) to reach the 'trachea.' RESULTS: Continuous nebulization from the ventilator position delivered significantly more aerosol (p < 0.00001) than did any other nebulzer position or mode. CONCLUSIONS: While the ventilator position of the nebulizer was the most effective, further studies are needed to determine whether changes in particle size through a long circuit result in more or less deposition of medication in large versus more peripheral airways. For this reason, in our institution we place the nebulizer at the manifold for routine administration of bronchodilators during MV. (Respir Care 1992;37:423-431.)

Introduction

It has been reported that only about 10% of the total dose from a medication nebulizer is deposited in the lung in nonintubated patients,[1,2] and only from 1.22%[3] to 4.8%[4] in intubated, mechanically

Mr Quinn is the Educational Coordinator, Respiratory Care Department, Ochsner Foundation Hospital, New Orleans, Louisiana.

A version of this paper was presented by Mr Quinn during the RESPIRATORY CARE OPEN FORUM at the 1991 AARC Annual Meeting held in Atlanta, Georgia.

Reprints: William W Quinn RPFT RRT, Respiratory Care, Ochsner Foundation Hospital, 1516 Jefferson Highway, New Orleans LA 70121.

ventilated patients. Furthermore, in the intubated patient, there can be no dose effect from oropharyngeal absorption, so the reduction in dose in the intubated patient may be even greater than this comparison suggests. To improve medication delivery from a nebulizer located in the ventilator circuit, one could try to titrate the medication dose upward until the desired effect was reached, but probably it is preferable to try to optimize the function of the nebulizer and circuit before giving unconventionally high doses of bronchodilators.

Intuitively, it might seem that a nebulizer placed at the patient Y-piece would be optimally situated to deliver the greatest percentage of the generated aerosol to the patient. However, Hughes and Saez,[5] in an in-vitro model, found that when the nebulizer was placed 90 cm back from the patient Y-piece (at the so-called manifold position), significantly more aerosol was directed toward the patient than when the nebulizer was placed in the conventional position at the patient Y-piece. They also studied the effect of continuous versus intermittent nebulization at the two nebulizer positions, finding that intermittent nebulization at the manifold position delivered significantly more of the generated aerosol than did any of the other methods studied.

I was influenced by the Hughes and Saez report to lobby for the movement of nebulizers from the Y-piece to the manifold position in our hospital. However, this idea was met with skepticism on the part of the staff, many of whom felt intuitively that the Y-piece position should be superior. It also came to light during discussion of this issue that many staff members were employing continuous flow to the nebulizer instead of the intermittent flow specified by our procedure manual and recommended by Hughes and Saez. In order to clarify this issue and help us settle on a consistent procedure, I decided to study the effects of nebulizer position and continuous versus intermittent flow with the equipment used in our hospital. Also, because Hughes and Saez[5] had suggested that the manifold position was superior to Y-piece placement of the nebulizer because the inspiratory tubing distal to the manifold became primed with aerosol, I wanted to try placing the nebulizer even farther back, at the ventilator end of the tubing, thus providing an even greater length of tubing to act as an aerosol reservoir.

Hughes and Saez had nebulized technetium through the delivery circuit to target filters, and had then radioscanned to determine the relative amounts of aerosol delivered in various tests. However, a scanning method was not immediately available to me. Instead, inspired by the urine dipstick tests I see around the hospital, I created a visual colorimetry method of determining aerosol delivery.

Materials and Methods

Methodology Overview

The general procedure was to run tests with the nebulizer at three different positions, with both continuous and intermittent nebulization at selected positions, in order to determine which combination of nebulizer position and nebulization mode would deliver the greatest amount of aerosol to the 'tracheal' end of an ETT. The nebulizer positions were (1) at the patient Y-piece, (2) at the manifold (90 cm back from the Y-piece), and (3) at the ventilator end of the inspiratory circuit (180 cm back from the Y-piece); this third location was the new position being tested. In each test, blue food coloring was nebulized for a certain period of time, with the aerosol being deposited on a yellow target (a bacteria filter) attached to the tracheal end of an ETT; the blue aerosol would change the filter's color to an extent proportional to the amount of aerosol that reached it—with light yellow-green colors representing lesser amounts, and darker blue-greens representing greater amounts. The target filters were then visually compared to a previously prepared color scale to determine, in a relative way, the amounts of aerosol reaching the targets when the nebulizer was in different positions, and operating either continuously or intermittently.

Some trials represented nebulization during controlled mechanical ventilation; other trials simulated nebulization in the presence of spontaneous ventilation in SIMV with pressure support (PS).

Colorimetry-Scale Preparation

Here the object was to create a stepped visual scale of 30 color values, representing delivery of aerosol from relatively small to relatively great amounts. The first step was to color 100 Marquest MQ-303 bacteria filters yellow. Each filter was attached to the T-piece on top of an Inspiron Intertech nebulizer, with the other side of the T-piece being capped. A 3-mL syringe was used to measure and place a dose of 0.5 mL of French's Yellow Food Coloring and 2.5 mL of normal saline in the nebulizer. The nebulizer was operated by oxygen flowing at 7 L/min from a Timeter TL016 flowmeter for a period of 2 minutes. The oxygen supply tubing was attached to and detached from the flowmeter for each run to assure that the flowmeter setting remained the same for all runs. Each run was timed with a Casio digital stopwatch. After the 100 filters had been colored yellow by this 2-minute exposure, they were allowed to dry for 2 days.

Next, a color scale was created by exposing each of 30 yellow filters to the nebulizer output, in the same manner as before, except that the nebulizer was loaded with 0.5 mL of French's Blue Food Coloring in 2.5 mL of normal saline, and the filters were exposed for different periods of time. Filter #1 was exposed for 5 seconds, Filter #2 for 10 seconds, and so on, with each filter receiving 5 more seconds of exposure than the one before it. Thus, 30 color-scale filters were generated, the first having been exposed to blue aerosol for 5 seconds, and the 30th for 150 seconds. The colors of the filter set progressed from a slight greening of the yellow base (Filter #1) to a dark blue-green (Filter #30).

The remaining yellow filters were available for use in tests of aerosol delivery in an in-vitro setup, after which they could be visually compared to the 30-step color scale.

Test Setup

Figure 1 diagrams the test setup, indicating a Puritan-Bennett 7200 ventilator at the bottom of the figure, with a Hudson 1613 circuit (showing the three nebulizer positions: ventilator, manifold, and Y-piece) connnected to the proximal end of the

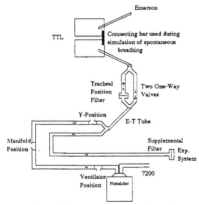

Fig. 1. The nebulizer test system, with Puritan-Bennett 7200 ventilator at bottom; ventilator circuit, showing the three nebulizer positions (ventilator position, manifold position, and Y-position); tracheal-position target filter; TTL test lung; and Emerson Post-Op ventilator.

ETT. A supplemental filter (Pall brand) was placed just proximal to the point of entry of exhaled gas into the heated expiratory filter subsystem, in order to protect the expiratory system of the ventilator from the colored aerosol. Ventilator settings used throughout testing were tidal volume 800 mL, rate 12/min, flow 50 L/min, with a square flow wave. The support arm was always in the same position, about a foot lower than the ETT connection, and the circuit had a 'droopy loop' between the support arm and the ventilator. Excess condensate was manually drained.

A Concha III humidifier was used, and temperature, monitored at the patient Y-piece, was maintained at 32°C until the begininng of each trial, at which time the humidifier was turned off and bypassed. It was turned on again and restabilized at 32°C between trials. This was done to provide a simulation of clinical conditions, while at the same time addressing concerns that the humidifier's low-temperature alarm might be actuated by the nebulizer flow, or that the continuation of humidification would have an adverse effect on aerosol stability.

The test filter was placed on a Y-piece attached to the distal ('tracheal') end of an 8-mm ETT. The ETT was clamped in a position such that the tracheal end of the ETT and the ventilator connector were at a 90-degree angle from each other, simulating the usual clinical configuration and its influence on aerosol delivery. One-way valves were employed so that inspiratory flow passed through the target filter on the way to the test lung, but expiratory flow was routed around the test filter on its way back to the ETT. The test lung was the left side of a two-chambered Michigan Instruments Training Test Lung (TTL).

Concern has been raised about the possibility that the target filter in such a bench test might receive condensed droplets draining from the ETT,[6] which would distort the results, as they would not be from aerosols that had reached this point. I addressed this in two ways. First, a freshly cleaned and dried ETT and associated adapters were used for each trial. Second, a dual-lumen adapter from a Baxter Isothermal neonatal ventilator circuit was employed at the tracheal end of the ETT to serve as a trap for condensate rolling down the lumen of the ETT.

In tests simulating spontaneous ventilation with pressure support (PS) in the SIMV mode, the left side of the test lung was linked to the right side by a footruler and a pair of clamps. The right side was then ventilated by an Emerson Post-Op ventilator at a rate of 20 breaths/min and a tidal volume of 400 mL. The Emerson was equipped with an IMV valve so that mechanical breaths to the left side of the TTL triggered by the movement of the lung would not be impaired by the limited extent of volume delivery (400 mL) to the right side.

Test Procedures

Blue food coloring and normal saline, as described, were placed in the nebulizer for each trial. Seven groups of trials were run.

Group 1: nebulizer at manifold position; continuous flow of oxygen to the nebulizer at 7 L/min for 6 min; 10 trials were run.

Group 2: nebulizer at manifold position; intermittent flow to nebulizer on inspiration only for 15 min; 10 trials.

Group 3: nebulizer at manifold position; intermittent flow to nebulizer on inspiration for 15 min; spontaneous ventilation with 10 cm H_2O PS added; 10 trials.

Group 4: nebulizer at ventilator position; continuous flow to nebulizer at 7 L/min for 6 min; 10 trials.

Group 5: nebulizer at ventilator position; continuous flow to nebulizer at 7 L/min for 6 min; spontaneous ventilation with 10 cm H_2O PS added; 10 trials.

Group 6: nebulizer at Y-piece; continuous flow to nebulizer at 7 L/min for 6 min; 5 trials.

Group 7: nebulizer at manifold; continuous flow to nebulizer at 7 L/min for 6 min; right angle on ventilator Y-piece removed in order to evaluate whether aerosol delivery changed due to a decrease in inertial impaction at this point; 5 trials. This part of the study was done because large blue droplets had formed inside the right-angle adapter in Group-1 trials, and I wanted to see whether more color reached the target filter if the right angle were not in the circuit.

Three additional filters were treated in the same manner as Filters 3, 6, and 12 of the colorimetry scale. They were mixed in with the test filters as a test of the reproducibility of the method.

The test filters were dried for 1 week, to allow differences caused by different drying times to subside. They were then numbered nonsequentially, and a jury of three persons not familiar with the test scored the filters against the 30-filter color scale. The jury was instructed to assign each test filter a single number, matching a color-scale number, to be reached by consensus.

Additional Tests

An additional set of measurements was made to elicit the difference in aerosol production when continuous versus intermittent nebulization was performed, and when circumstances used by Hughes and Saez[5] were compared with different circumstances that I considered to be closer to clinical conditions.

Four different models of nebulizer (Hudson 1782, Intertech 7763, Bennett TwinJet, and Bennett Raindrop) were tested in four different circumstances: (1) continuous nebulization for 3 minutes (method of Hughes and Saez[5]), (2) continuous nebulization for 6 minutes, (3) intermittent nebulization for 17 minutes with flowrate set at 50 L/min, and (4) intermittent nebulization for 17 minutes with flow adjusted to give an I:E of 1:3 (method of Hughes and Saez). The nebulizers were at the manifold position. Five trials of each circumstance were run for each nebulizer.

Statistical Analysis

A one-way analysis of covariance[7] was performed, and p < 0.05 was to be considered statistically significant.

Results

Table 1 lists the color scores for all the trials, group by group. Both Group 4 (nebulizer at ventilator position, continuous flow) and Group 5 (nebulizer at ventilator position, continuous flow, spontaneous ventilation and PS) had significantly higher scores than all other groups (p < 0.00001), indicating that significantly greater amounts of aerosol reached the 'trachea' when the nebulizer was at the ventilator position with continuous flow. Figure 2 illustrates this graphically.

Table 1. Results of Colorimetric Determination of Aerosol Deposition under Seven Conditions

Group 1	Group 2	Group 3	Group 4	Group 5	Group 6	Group 7
8	2	4	11	11	6	8
9	2	5	12	12	4	8
7	2	5	12	13	4	7
7	1	5	12	13	5	8
8	2	6	11	14	5	8
9	2	4	12	12		
8	2	5	11	14		
8	2	5	12	14		
9	2	4	13	12		
9	1	6	12	13		
Mean (SD)						
8.2	1.8	4.9	11.8	12.8	4.8	8.0
(0.79)	(0.42)	(0.74)	(0.63)	(1.03)	(0.8)	(0.75)

* Group 1 = nebulizer at manifold; continuous flow at 7 L/min for 6 min.

Group 2 = nebulizer at manifold; intermittent flow on inspiration for 15 min.

Group 3 = nebulizer at manifold; intermittent flow on inspiration for 15 min + 10 cm H_2O pressure support with spontaneous ventilation.

Group 4 = nebulizer at ventilator; continuous flow at 7 L/min for 6 min.

Group 5 = nebulizer at ventilator; continuous flow at 7 L/min for 6 min + 10 cm H_2O pressure support with spontaneous ventilation.

Group 6 = nebulizer at Y-piece; continuous flow at 7 L/min for 6 min.

Group 7 = nebulizer at manifold; continuous flow at 7 L/min for 6 min; right angle on Y-piece removed to see whether this affected aerosol delivery.

In Group 7, removal of the right angle did not increase the delivery of aerosol to the target filter, as judged by visual colorimetry.

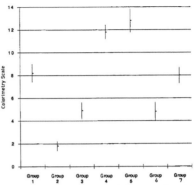

Fig. 2. Mean and 1 standard deviation ranges for color scores in the seven nebulization test groups.

The three extra filters mixed in with the test filters as controls were all correctly matched with their twins (#3, #6, #12), confirming the reliability of the visual colorimetry method.

Table 2 gives the results of the additional tests with four different models of nebulizer. This simply illustrates the fact that far more medication leaves the nebulizer in 6 minutes of continuous nebulization than in 17 minutes of intermittent nebulization ($p < 0.00001$).

Discussion

The results from Group 6 (nebulizer at Y-piece, continuous flow) and from Group 1 (nebulizer at

Table 2. Weight Loss of Four Models of Nebulizers under Four Test Conditions

Test Conditions*	Hudson 1782	Intertech 7763	Bennett TwinJet	Bennett Raindrop
Continuous nebulization for 3 min	0.54 (0.04)†	0.78 (0.03)	0.32 (0.03)	0.49 (0.05)
Continuous nebulization for 6 min	0.91 (0.06)	1.27 (0.06)	0.61 (0.02)	0.84 (0.04)
Intermittent nebulization for 17 min @ 50 L/min flow	0.48 (0.02)	0.49 (0.04)	0.26 (0.01)	0.42 (0.03)
Intermittent nebulization for 17 min with flowrate adjusted to provide I:E of 1:3	0.60 (0.04)	0.62 (0.05)	0.27 (0.02)	0.52 (0.05)

*n = 5 trials/nebulizer.

† Mean (SD) in grams.

manifold, continuous flow) provide a qualitative confirmation of the findings of Hughes and Saez[5] that a nebulizer at the manifold is much more efficient than a nebulizer at the Y-piece—when the nebulizer is run continuously. However, my study of intermittent flow with the nebulizer at the manifold position (Group 2) failed to confirm the Hughes and Saez finding that intermittent nebulization was superior to continuous nebulization in delivering medication. In fact, my data lead to the opposite conclusion.

The reasons for this difference lie in four designed differences between my methods and those of Hughes and Saez. The first difference, my use of visual colorimetry rather than radioassay, was dictated by circumstance. The other three differences in methodology resulted from my attempts to make the model more closely reflect ICU conditions. First, I employed heated humidity;* second, I interposed an ETT between the circuit and the lung model; and, third, my continuous nebulization runs lasted 6 minutes instead of the 3 minutes that Hughes and Saez employed, and my intermittent runs lasted 15 minutes rather than the 17 minutes that theirs did. This last difference is obviously the most important.

Hughes and Saez studied what percentage of a given quantity of aerosol was directed toward the patient. In order to do this, they estimated, based on serial weighings of the nebulizer, that equivalent quantities of matter left the nebulizer in the form of aerosol in a period of 3 minutes during continuous nebulization and in 17 minutes during intermittent nebulization. The problem with this is that, whereas 15 to 17 minutes is probably the upper practical time limit for duration of medication delivery[8] in most instances, there is no practical barrier to continuing to operate a nebulizer on continuous flow beyond 3 minutes, all the way until the medication is exhausted. I limited my test to 6 minutes because the nebulizer I used begins to sputter and give uneven output at 6 minutes; however, for a realistic trial of methods, there is no reason I could not have run both forms of nebulization

* Hughes and Saez[5] show a Cascade I humidifier in the inspiratory side in their figure. However, John Hughes told me (telephone conversation, October 1988) that this was shown only to clarify which was the inspiratory side; the trials themselves were run dry.

for 10 minutes and compared total delivery at that point. Given appropriate positioning of the nebulizer in the ventilator circuit, it is clear that total drug delivery to the patient by continuous nebulization would far exceed that delivered by intermittent nebulization during inspiration only, if a standard time of administration of 10 or 15 minutes were desired.

To further address this point, I performed studies to see how much weight the nebulizer loses when operated intermittently for 17 minutes and when operated continuously for 3 minutes, which were the times used by Hughes and Saez, as well as how much it loses when operated continuously for 6 minutes, which was the time I used in the position phase of my study. As seen in Table 2, the nebulizer brand affects results. The Puritan-Bennett Raindrop, which Hughes and Saez used, does indeed nebulize about the same amount in 17 minutes of intermittent operation as in 3 minutes of continuous operation as they reported. The fact that I used an Intertech 7763, which nebulizes less in 17 minutes of intermittent operation than in 3 minutes of continuous operation has obviously increased differences between the findings of the two studies, but the deliberate choice of and importance of the time period remains dominant. One other point to be made here is that, as shown in Table 2, duplicating Hughes and Saez's adjustment of flow to provide an I:E of 1:3 could have improved the intermittent nebulization performance of my Intertech nebulizer (because of the longer inspiratory time), but doing this would have brought the ventilator flowrate down to around the 35-L/min range, which is probably not appropriate in the adult ICU in most instances.[9]

The data on intermittent nebulization performance appear to conflict with the observation of Fuller et al[3] that after 15 minutes of nebulization on inspiration only, "usually only the 0.5 mL 'dead' volume remained" (they used a Puritan-Bennett TwinJet nebulizer). The ventilators in their study included the MA-1 and BEAR 2, which nebulize only on volume-cycled breaths when intermittent nebulization is employed, and the ventilator settings were not reported. In view of the fact that no serial weighings of the nebulizer were reported, it seems likely to me that the quantity of medication remaining in the nebulizer was much greater than was appreciated, particularly as they used the Twinjet nebulizer, which my findings (Table 2) indicate nebulizes out more slowly than other commonly used models.

A hypothetical ranking of the efficiency of the seven nebulization methods I studied is given in Figure 3. This assumes that the color-scale filters reflect 100% efficiency for the time period that they were exposed to nebulizer output. A ratio between nebulizer output in volume for that time period (based on timed weighings of the nebulizer, which indicated that approximately 0.01 mL of solution nebulized out every 5 seconds) and the total volume of solution in the nebulizer should reflect an approximation of the total efficiency of the nebulization method. Although these percentages are hypothetical, they are consistent with the studies of Fuller et al[3] and Fraser et al,[4] which showed reductions in aerosol delivery in intubated patients, even when nebulizer performance was optimized. This supports the policy of those hospitals that have elected to double bronchodilator concentrations when nebulizing medication to the ventilated patient.

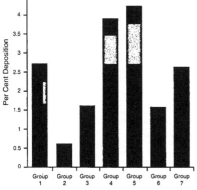

Fig. 3. Hypothetical efficiency (% deposition) of aerosol delivery of the seven nebulization test groups.

Dahlbäck et al[10] described a method of nebulizing on expiration only, which is similar to continuous nebulization in that the inspiratory tubing is primed with mist in both methods. The concept of expiratory nebulization is intriguing because, if fur-

ther developed by ventilator manufacturers, it might offer a method of using nebulizers effectively without adversely affecting the operation of the ventilator. The immediate relevance of Dahlbäck et al's study is that they point out that with the expiratory nebulization method, you must note whether the tubing between the nebulizer and the patient connnection is completely filled with mist during the expiratory period. If it is not so filled (because the nebulizer is too far back from the patient), the first part of the tidal volume will not carry medication; although the total medication delivery will be good, it is likely that more medication will be deposited in the large airways than in the lung periphery.

Continuous nebulization with the nebulizer in the ventilator position does not duplicate Dahlbäck et al's scenario, because the nebulizer runs during both inspiration and expiration. With continuous flow, the part of the tubing charged with mist during expiration may have a greater density of mist than the part charged during inspiration, due to the difference in flow levels of respiratory gas passing the nebulizer; nevertheless, there will be some amount of mist throughout the tubing between the nebulizer and the patient, regardless of the nebulizer position. The situation is further complicated when the patient is breathing spontaneously in the IMV mode. Further study of nebulizer position by a radioassay method would be helpful in determining regional lung deposition of the aerosol. Because of this unresolved question about regional deposition, in our hospital we are using continuous nebulization with the nebulizer at the manifold position as our standard nebulization protocol.

Another aspect of this is the well-known concern about changes in particle size when a mist passes through the circuit in this way.[11] I have no means of studying the particle size of the mist after it traverses the ventilator circuit, whether for a distance of 90 or 180 cm, but the fact that the mist has passed the ETT in the model in the presence of a wet circuit is encouraging.

The ventilator position and continuous nebulization appear to offer an advantage over previously studied methods. It seems worth noting that in the dose-response portion of the study by MacIntyre et al[2]—and in the study by Gay et al[12]—the nebulizer appears to have been in the position closest to the patient, and it was operated continuously.* As I interpret the data of Hughes and Saez,[5] moving the nebulizer back to the manifold position would have doubled the dose delivery under the conditions used by MacIntyre et al[2] and by Gay et al.[12] According to the results of my study, even greater improvement could come from moving the nebulizer back to the ventilator end of the circuit. Making cross-study comparisons of this kind is very hazardous, but it does seem that the whole tale is not yet told.

The fact that continuous flow appears needed to operate a ventilator nebulizer effectively within a reasonable period of time means that the nebulizer method employed is inextricably linked to the well-known associated problems of increased tidal volume, disabled expiratory monitors, impaired sensitivity, and cycling of pressure support that come from the use of continuous flow to a nebulizer. This is in addition to the possibility of contamination common to all small-volume nebulizers.[13] More than one manufacturer has issued a warning that continuous-flow nebulization should not be employed with their ventilators.†‡ This leads to the conclusion that routine bronchodilator administration in the adult ICU should be accomplished by metered dose inhaler (MDI), as has been suggested.[13] However, this change has not been accomplished in my institution—or, I believe, in many others.

On the other hand, when medications such as antibiotics are given, where the MDI is not an option, nebulization from the ventilator position with continuous flow may well be worth consideration. Furthermore, some institutions may use ventilators whose manufacturers have not recommended against continuous nebulization, or they may have other reasons for continuing to use nebulizers in preference to MDIs.

Since performing this investigation, I have discovered that the ventilator position for the neb-

ulizer has previously been used, particularly where heated-wire circuits were used that could not be broken into at the manifold position. Further research may be indicated to benefit these practitioners, both to determine regional lung deposition and to compare the effects of various conditions of humidification. In addition, the visual colorimetry method that has been described here may be of interest to educators as a laboratory exercise for students.

Conclusions

While in this study the ventilator position of the nebulizer was the most effective for delivering aerosol to the filter at the tracheal end of the endotracheal tube, concerns about possible changes in aerosol particle size through the long circuit require further studies be performed (including radioassay studies of regional reginal lung deposition) before the question of optimal nebulizer placement in MV circuits can be settled. For these reasons, in our institution we are placing the nebulizer at the manifold position for routine administration of bronchodilators during MV.

ACKNOWLEDGMENTS

The author thanks Ahmed Abduh PhD, Ochsner Research Division, for statistical consultation.

PRODUCT SOURCES

Endotracheal Tube:
Intertech/Ohio, Intertech Resources, Bannockburn IL

Food Coloring:
French's Food Coloring, RT French, Rochester NY

Bacteria Filters:
Pall HME 15-22, Pall Biomedical Inc, Fajardo PR
Marquest MQ-303, Marquest Medical Products, Englewood CO

Flowmeter:
Timeter TL016, Allied Healthcare Products Inc, St Louis MO

Humidifier:
Conchatherm III, Hudson RCI, Temecula CA

Nebulizers:
Bennett Raindrop, Puritan-Bennett Corp, Overland Park KS
Bennett TwinJet, Puritan-Bennett Corp, Overland Park KS
Hudson 1782, Hudson RCI, Temecula CA
Intertech 7763, Intertech Resources, Lincolnshire IL

---

* It is not clear from Gay et al's paper whether nebulization was intermittent or continuous; however, Gay clarified to me (telephone conversation, May 1991) that it was continuous.

† Fitzpatrick D. IRISA ventilator. A PPG Seminar. New Orleans LA: PPG, November 7, 1991.

‡ Niles D. Medical device information: a letter from Puritan-Bennett. August 29, 1990.

Balance:
Mettler Model PM 480 Deltarange, Mettler Instrument Corp, Hightstown NJ

Test Lung:
Michigan TTL, Michigan Instruments Inc, Grand Rapids MI

Ventilators:
Emerson Post-Op, JH Emerson Co, Cambridge MA
Puritan-Bennett 7200, Puritan-Bennett Corp, Overland Park KS

Ventilator Circuit:
Hudson 1613, Hudson RCI, Temecula CA

Statistical Software:
BMDP 2V, BMDP, Los Angeles CA

REFERENCES

1. Lewis RA, Fleming JS. Fractional deposition from a jet nebulizer: how it differs from a metered dose inhaler. Br J Dis Chest 1985;79:361-367.
2. MacIntyre NR, Silver RM, Miller CW, Schuler F, Coleman RE. Aerosol delivery in intubated, mechanically ventilated patients. Crit Care Med 1985;13:81-84.
3. Fuller HD, Dolovich MB, Posmituck G, Wong Pack W, Newhouse MT. Pressurized aerosol versus jet aerosol delivery to mechanically ventilated patients: comparison of dose to the lungs. Am Rev Respir Dis 1990;141:440-444.
4. Fraser I, Duvall A, Dolovich M, Newhouse MT. Therapeutic aerosol delivery in ventilator systems (abstract). Am Rev Respir Dis 1981;123(4, Part 2):107.
5. Hughes J, Saez J. Effects of nebulizer mode and position in a mechanical ventilator circuit on dose efficiency. Respir Care 1987;32:1131-1135.
6. Ahrens RC, Ries RA, Popendorf W, Wiese JA. The delivery of therapeutic aerosols through endotracheal tubes. Pediatr Pulmonol 1986;2(1):19-26.
7. Kirkwood BR. Essentials of medical statistics. Cambridge MA: Blackwell Scientific Publications, 1988:41-45.
8. Hess D, Horney D, Snyder T. Medication-delivery performance of eight small-volume, hand-held nebulizers: effects of diluent volume, gas flowrate, and nebulizer model. Respir Care 1989;34:717-723.
9. Marini JJ, Capps JS, Culver BH. The inspiratory work of breathing during assisted mechanical ventilation. Chest 1985;87:612-618.
10. Dahlbäck M, Wollmer P, Drefeldt B, Jonson B. Controlled aerosol delivery during mechanical ventilation. J Aerosol Med 1989;2(4):339-347.
11. Phipps PR, Gonda I. Droplets produced by medical nebulizers: some factors affecting their size and solute concentration. Chest 1990; 97:1327-1332.
12. Gay PC, Patel HG, Nelson SB, Gilles B, Hubmayr RD. Metered dose inhalers for bronchodilator delivery in intubated, mechanically ventilated patients. Chest 1991; 99:66-71.
13. Hess D. How should bronchodilators be administered to patients on ventilators? Respir Care 1991;36:377-394.

CORRECTIONS

Variations in Tidal Volume with Portable Transport Ventilators (Respir Care 1992;37:233-239)

The last sentence of Column 1 on Page 239 should read "The AutoVent 3000 and the Bird Mini-TXP delivered a V_T less than 80% of control under the worst conditions of pulmonary mechanics. The AutoVent 3000 delivered 78% of control while the Bird Mini-TXP delivered only 40% of control."

Transcutaneous P_{CO_2} and End-Tidal P_{CO_2} in Ventilated Adults (Respir Care 1992;37:240-248)

In Table 2, P_{etCO_2} vs P_{aCO_2} bias should be –5.13, rather than 5.13, and Figures 1B and 2A were switched.

We regret the errors.

An Evaluation of the Resistance to Flow through the Patient Valves of Twelve Adult Manual Resuscitators

Dean Hess MEd RRT and Mark Simmons MSed RPFT RRT

STUDY QUESTION: What is the inspiratory and expiratory resistance to flow through the patient valves of adult manual resuscitators? MATERIALS & METHODS: We evaluated the resistance to flow through the patient valves of 12 adult resuscitators (Ambu, Code Blue, DMR, Hope 4, Hospitak, Hudson, Intertech, Laerdal, Mercury, Respironics, SPUR, Vitalograph). Expiratory resistance was evaluated by directing a flow of oxygen through the valve in the direction that the patient expires. Inspiratory resistance was evaluated by directing oxygen through the valve in the direction of flow when the bag is squeezed. Flow was controlled by a Timeter 0-75 flowmeter, and measured using a calibrated Timeter RT-200. Flows of 10, 20, 30, 40, 50, 60, 70, 80, and 90 L/min were used. Resistive back pressure of the resuscitator valves was measured using a calibrated Timeter RT-200. Resistance was calculated by dividing back pressure by flow. Five measurements were made at each flow setting for each resuscitator. RESULTS: Significant differences in back pressures and resistances existed between the resuscitators for both expiratory and inspiratory flows (p < 0.001 in each case). Significant interaction effects also existed between resuscitator brands and flows (p < 0.001 in each case). At an expiratory flow of 50 L/min, all resuscitators except the Hospitak and Vitalograph produced a back pressure < 5 cm H_2O (the International Standards Organization standard). At an inspiratory flow of 50 L/min, all resuscitators but the Hospitak, Mercury, and Vitalograph produced a back pressure < 5 cm H_2O. CONCLUSIONS: Significant differences existed in the back pressures produced due to the flow resistance through the patient valves of these resuscitators, and these might be considered excessive in some cases. Because this was a bench study, further work is needed to determine the clinical importance of these findings. (Respir Care 1992;37:432-438.)

Introduction

Manual (bag-valve) resuscitators are commonly used during cardiopulmonary resuscitation. They are also used to provide ventilation during the

Mr Hess is Assistant Director. Department of Research. York Hospital, and Instructor, School of Respiratory Therapy. and Mr Simmons is Program Director. School of Respiratory Therapy—York Hospital and York College of Pennsylvania. York, Pennsylvania.

A version of this paper was presented by Mr Simmons during the RESPIRATORY CARE OPEN FORUM at the 1991 AARC Annual Meeting held in Atlanta. Georgia.

Reprints: Dean Hess. Department of Research, York Hospital. 1001 South George St, York PA 17405.

transport of apneic patients and during endotracheal suctioning. Various aspects of the performance of manual resuscitators have been published in the past 10 years: comparison of volumes delivered by bag-valve-mask, mouth-to-mouth. mouth-to-mask, and portable ventilators;[1-4] volumes delivered using one hand versus two hands to squeeze the bag;[5-7] volumes delivered wearing gloves versus not wearing gloves;[8] volumes delivered with various hand sizes;[6] volumes delivered with various brands of resuscitators;[6,8] performance at extremes of environmental conditions;[9] and compliance of commercial brands of resuscitators to standards published by the American Society for Testing and Materials (ASTM).[10,11] To our knowledge, very little has been published related to the resistance to flow through the valves of manual resuscitators. Excessive expiratory resistance through the resuscitator valve could result in prolonged exhalation and air-trapping (auto-PEEP). Excessive inspiratory resistance could result in hand fatigue for the person squeezing the bag, and could also affect the patient's ability to inspire spontaneously through the valve. The International Standards Organization (ISO) has recommended that the back pressure through the valve of the resuscitator should not exceed 5 cm H_2O at a flow of 50 L/min.[12] We conducted this study to evaluate the resistance to flow through the patient valves of 12 commercially available adult manual resuscitators at flows of 10-90 L/min.

Materials and Methods

We evaluated the patient valves of the following adult manual resuscitators:* Ambu Mark III, Vital Signs Code Blue, Puritan-Bennett Disposable Manual Resuscitator (DMR), Matrx Medical Hope 4, Hospitak Manual Pulmonary Resuscitator, Hudson Lifesaver Manual Resuscitator, Intertech Safe Response, Laerdal Adult Resuscitator, Mercury CPR, Respironics Adult BagEasy with PEEP valve (PEEP set at zero for all testing), Ambu SPUR, and Vitalograph. All resuscitators were tested new, as supplied by the manufacturer.

Inspiratory Resistance

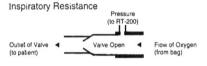

Expiratory Resistance

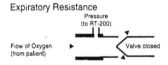

Fig. 1. Inspiratory resistance was measured by directing flow through the valve in the direction of flow when the bag is squeezed; expiratory resistance was measured by directing flow through the valve in the direction of flow when the patient exhales. This generic valve is intended to illustrate the test setup used for the patient, and does not represent any commercially available device.

Expiratory resistance was evaluated by directing a flow of oxygen through the valve in the direction of flow when the patient exhales (Fig. 1). Inspiratory resistance was evaluated by directing a flow of oxygen through the valve in the direction of flow when the bag is squeezed (Fig. 1). Flow was controlled by a Timeter 0-75 flowmeter and measured with a calibrated Timeter RT-200. Flows of 10, 20, 30, 40, 50, 60, 70, 80, and 90 L/min were used. Resistive back pressure was measured using a calibrated Timeter RT-200. Resistance was calculated by dividing back pressure by flow. The methodology was similar to in-vitro constant-flow methods that have been used to evaluate resistive pressure through ventilator exhalation valves,[13] PEEP valves,[14] and endotracheal tubes.[15] Five measurements were made at each flow setting for each resuscitator.

Mean and standard deviation (SD) were determined for each resuscitator at each flow for the inspiratory and expiratory directions. Two-way analysis of variance was performed for inspiratory and expiratory flows, using resuscitator brand (12 levels) and flow (9 levels) as factors. Post-hoc analysis was conducted using the Scheffe procedure to determine statistically significant differences between pairs of resuscitators ($p < 0.05$ was considered significant). All statistical analysis was performed using commercially available statistical software, and standard methodology.[16]

Results

Mean (SD) data are tabulated in Tables 1 and 2. There were significant differences between the resuscitators for back pressure and resistance with both the inspiratory and expiratory flows ($p < 0.001$, in each case). There were also significant interaction effects between resuscitator brands and flows for back pressure and resistance in both the inspiratory and expiratory directions ($p < 0.001$, in each case). Results of post-hoc Scheffe analyses are tabulated in Tables 3 and 4. The inspiratory and expiratory back pressures at a flow of 50 L/min (according to the ISO standard) are shown in Figure 2.

---

* Manufacturers are identified in the Product Sources section at the end of the text.

Discussion

To our knowledge, this is the first reported study to evaluate the inspiratory and expiratory resistive back pressures through adult resuscitator valves. Although we found differences in the back pres-

sures and resistances between the resuscitators that we evaluated, most met the ISO standard of back pressure less than 5 cm H_2O at a flow of 50 L/min.[12] The Hospitak and Vitalograph did not meet the ISO standard for both inspiratory and expiratory flows, and the Mercury did not meet the ISO

Table 1. Back Pressures as a Function of Flow for the Adult Manual Resuscitators Evaluated in this Study

					Flows (L/min)				
	10	20	30	40	50	60	70	80	90
Ambu									
expiratory	0.7 (0.02)*	1.1 (0.02)	1.5 (0.01)	2.0 (0.01)	2.5 (0.03)	3.1 (0.04)	3.7 (0.02)	4.5 (0.01)	5.3 (0.02)
inspiratory	0.9 (0.01)	1.3 (0.01)	1.7 (0.09)	2.1 (0.01)	2.6 (0.01)	3.1 (0.01)	3.7 (0.01)	4.3 (0.01)	5.0 (0.01)
Code Blue									
expiratory	0.3 (0.05)	0.6 (0.03)	0.8 (0.03)	1.1 (0.02)	1.4 (0.01)	1.9 (0.02)	2.5 (0.01)	3.1 (0.01)	3.9 (0.03)
inspiratory	0.8 (0.03)	1.5 (0.03)	2.1 (0.03)	2.8 (0.03)	3.5 (0.03)	4.2 (0.03)	5.0 (0.03)	5.9 (0.02)	6.9 (0.03)
DMR									
expiratory	0.1 (0.01)	0.3 (0.01)	0.6 (0.01)	1.1 (0.01)	1.6 (0.01)	2.3 (0.01)	3.1 (0.01)	4.0 (0.01)	5.0 (0.01)
inspiratory	0.7 (0.01)	1.6 (0.01)	2.5 (0.03)	3.7 (0.02)	4.9 (0.02)	6.4 (0.06)	8.1 (0.06)	9.6 (0.02)	11.5 (0.19)
Hope 4									
expiratory	1.5 (0.03)	2.3 (0.02)	2.7 (0.02)	3.1 (0.02)	1.7 (0.06)	2.0 (0.03)	2.3 (0.03)	2.6 (0.03)	3.0 (0.06)
inspiratory	0.8 (0.01)	1.0 (0.01)	1.4 (0.01)	1.9 (0.01)	2.4 (0.02)	3.0 (0.01)	3.6 (0.02)	4.4 (0.02)	5.4 (0.01)
Hospitak									
expiratory	1.8 (0.01)	2.5 (0.04)	4.0 (0.03)	5.6 (0.02)	7.4 (0.02)	9.2 (0.02)	11.2 (0.02)	13.2 (0.03)	15.6 (0.03)
inspiratory	2.7 (0.06)	4.6 (0.06)	6.1 (0.07)	7.7 (0.05)	9.1 (0.05)	10.6 (0.04)	12.2 (0.05)	13.8 (0.07)	15.6 (0.16)
Hudson									
expiratory	0.4 (0.02)	0.7 (0.03)	1.0 (0.05)	1.4 (0.06)	1.9 (0.02)	2.4 (0.07)	2.9 (0.08)	3.3 (0.09)	3.9 (0.04)
inspiratory	1.0 (0.04)	1.7 (0.04)	2.2 (0.03)	2.8 (0.03)	3.3 (0.03)	4.0 (0.04)	4.5 (0.03)	5.2 (0.03)	6.0 (0.03)
Intertech									
expiratory	0.4 (0.01)	1.3 (0.01)	2.0 (0.02)	2.8 (0.02)	3.4 (0.01)	4.0 (0.01)	4.5 (0.01)	5.0 (0.01)	5.4 (0.02)
inspiratory	1.2 (0.04)	2.0 (0.03)	2.8 (0.03)	3.6 (0.03)	4.4 (0.02)	5.3 (0.02)	6.1 (0.05)	7.1 (0.02)	8.0 (0.05)
Laerdal									
expiratory	0.6 (0.04)	1.1 (0.05)	1.5 (0.01)	2.0 (0.02)	2.4 (0.03)	3.0 (0.04)	3.4 (0.07)	3.9 (0.02)	4.4 (0.08)
inspiratory	0.8 (0.05)	1.4 (0.05)	1.9 (0.04)	2.5 (0.02)	3.1 (0.06)	3.8 (0.04)	4.6 (0.04)	5.5 (0.03)	6.3 (0.04)
Mercury									
expiratory	0.4 (0.01)	0.9 (0.01)	1.7 (0.01)	2.5 (0.01)	3.3 (0.02)	4.2 (0.02)	5.2 (0.03)	6.0 (0.05)	6.9 (0.04)
inspiratory	1.6 (0.01)	2.8 (0.02)	3.9 (0.02)	4.9 (0.01)	6.1 (0.01)	7.3 (0.01)	8.6 (0.02)	9.9 (0.02)	11.2 (0.03)
Respironics									
expiratory	1.3 (0.03)	1.8 (0.03)	2.0 (0.03)	2.4 (0.05)	2.6 (0.04)	2.9 (0.03)	3.1 (0.03)	3.2 (0.05)	3.4 (0.02)
inspiratory	1.2 (0.02)	1.8 (0.02)	2.4 (0.06)	2.9 (0.03)	3.5 (0.03)	4.1 (0.04)	4.7 (0.02)	5.4 (0.02)	6.2 (0.02)
SPUR									
expiratory	0.1 (0.01)	0.4 (0.02)	0.8 (0.03)	1.4 (0.05)	2.0 (0.06)	2.8 (0.07)	3.6 (0.08)	4.7 (0.05)	5.9 (0.06)
inspiratory	0.3 (0.04)	0.4 (0.04)	0.6 (0.01)	1.0 (0.02)	1.3 (0.02)	1.8 (0.04)	2.4 (0.05)	3.1 (0.06)	3.8 (0.10)
Vitalograph									
expiratory	1.1 (0.24)	3.7 (0.28)	6.8 (0.25)	8.8 (0.92)	9.9 (1.12)	10.4 (0.83)	10.8 (1.06)	10.4 (1.24)	10.8 (1.68)
inspiratory	1.9 (0.03)	3.7 (0.14)	5.9 (0.06)	8.3 (0.06)	10.7 (0.13)	13.2 (0.06)	15.7 (0.13)	18.0 (0.08)	20.5 (0.12)

*All values are mean (SD) in cm H_2O.

Table 2.   Resistances as a Function of Flow for the Adult Manual Resuscitators Evaluated in this Study

	Flows (L/min)								
	10	20	30	40	50	60	70	80	90
Ambu									
expiratory	4.3 (0.17)*	3.2 (0.06)	3.0 (0.02)	3.0 (0.01)	3.0 (0.04)	3.1 (0.04)	3.2 (0.02)	3.4 (0.01)	3.6 (0.01)
inspiratory	5.3 (0.04)	4.0 (0.01)	3.5 (0.17)	3.2 (0.01)	3.2 (0.02)	3.1 (0.01)	3.2 (0.01)	3.2 (0.01)	3.3 (0.01)
Code Blue									
expiratory	2.0 (0.31)	1.7 (0.10)	1.6 (0.05)	1.7 (0.03)	1.7 (0.01)	1.9 (0.02)	2.1 (0.01)	2.4 (0.01)	2.5 (0.02)
inspiratory	4.9 (0.18)	4.5 (0.10)	4.3 (0.06)	4.1 (0.04)	4.2 (0.03)	4.2 (0.03)	4.3 (0.03)	4.4 (0.02)	4.5 (0.02)
DMR									
expiratory	0.5 (0.01)	0.9 (0.02)	1.2 (0.01)	1.6 (0.01)	1.9 (0.01)	2.3 (0.01)	2.6 (0.01)	3.0 (0.01)	3.3 (0.01)
inspiratory	4.3 (0.03)	4.7 (0.01)	5.1 (0.05)	5.6 (0.03)	5.9 (0.03)	6.4 (0.06)	6.9 (0.05)	7.2 (0.02)	7.7 (0.12)
Hope 4									
expiratory	8.8 (0.18)	7.0 (0.07)	5.4 (0.04)	4.7 (0.04)	2.0 (0.07)	2.0 (0.07)	2.0 (0.03)	1.9 (0.02)	2.0 (0.04)
inspiratory	4.6 (0.01)	3.0 (0.04)	2.7 (0.01)	2.8 (0.02)	2.9 (0.02)	3.0 (0.01)	3.1 (0.02)	3.3 (0.01)	3.6 (0.01)
Hospitak									
expiratory	11.2 (0.08)	7.4 (0.12)	8.0 (0.05)	8.4 (0.03)	8.9 (0.03)	9.2 (0.02)	9.6 (0.02)	10.0 (0.02)	10.4 (0.11)
inspiratory	16.1 (0.3)	13.8 (0.2)	12.2 (0.1)	11.5 (0.1)	11.0 (0.1)	10.6 (0.1)	10.5 (0.1)	10.4 (0.1)	10.4 (0.1)
Hudson									
expiratory	2.2 (0.12)	2.1 (0.09)	2.0 (0.11)	2.1 (0.09)	2.2 (0.02)	2.4 (0.07)	2.4 (0.07)	2.5 (0.07)	2.6 (0.03)
inspiratory	5.8 (0.25)	5.0 (0.12)	4.4 (0.06)	4.1 (0.05)	4.0 (0.04)	4.0 (0.04)	3.9 (0.03)	3.9 (0.02)	4.0 (0.02)
Intertech									
expiratory	2.9 (0.05)	3.8 (0 03)	4 0 (0.03)	4.1 (0.02)	4.1 (0.01)	4.0 (0.01)	3.9 (0.01)	3.6 (0.01)	3.6 (0.01)
inspiratory	7.1 (0.24)	6.0 (0.08)	5.6 (0.07)	5.4 (0.04)	5.3 (0.03)	5.3 (0.02)	5.3 (0.03)	5.2 (0.02)	5.3 (0.03)
Laerdal									
expiratory	3.8 (0.25)	3.2 (0.15)	3.0 (0.03)	3.0 (0.03)	2.9 (0.04)	3.0 (0.04)	2.9 (0.06)	2.9 (0.02)	2.9 (0.05)
inspiratory	4.7 (0.28)	4.2 (0.14)	3.8 (0.08)	3.8 (0.03)	3.7 (0.08)	3.8 (0.04)	4.0 (0.03)	4.1 (0.02)	4.2 (0.02)
Mercury									
expiratory	2.6 (0.03)	2.7 (0.04)	3.4 (0.03)	3.7 (0.01)	4.0 (0.03)	4.2 (0.01)	4.4 (0.03)	4.5 (0.04)	4.6 (0.02)
inspiratory	9.3 (0.07)	8.3 (0.06)	7.7 (0.04)	7.4 (0.01)	7.3 (0.01)	7.3 (0.01)	7.3 (0.01)	7.4 (0.02)	7.4 (0.02)
Respironics									
expiratory	8.0 (0.20)	5.4 (0.10)	4.0 (0.10)	3.5 (0.08)	3.2 (0.05)	2.9 (0.03)	2.6 (0.03)	2.4 (0.04)	2.3 (0.01)
inspiratory	7.1 (0.09)	5.3 (0.05)	4.8 (0.12)	4.4 (0.05)	4.2 (0.04)	4.1 (0.04)	4.1 (0.01)	4.1 (0.01)	4.1 (0.01)
SPUR									
expiratory	0.6 (0.03)	1.2 (0.05)	1.6 (0.07)	2.0 (0.08)	2.4 (0.07)	2.8 (0.07)	3.1 (0.06)	3.5 (0.04)	3.9 (0.04)
inspiratory	1.6 (0.24)	1.2 (0.13)	1.3 (0.01)	1.4 (0.01)	1.6 (0.03)	1.8 (0.04)	2.1 (0.05)	2.3 (0.04)	2.5 (0.04)
Vitalograph									
expiratory	6.4 (1.45)	11.1 (0.8)	13.5 (0.5)	13.1 (1.4)	11.9 (1.3)	10.4 (0.8)	9.2 (0.91)	7.8 (0.93)	7.2 (1.11)
inspiratory	11.4 (0.2)	11.0 (0.4)	11.8 (0.1)	12.4 (0.1)	12.8 (0.2)	13.2 (0.1)	13.4 (0.1)	13.5 (0.1)	13.7 (0.1)

*All values are mean (SD) in cm $H_2O \cdot s \cdot L^{-1}$.

standard for inspiratory flow. Using the American Heart Association criteria of a tidal volume of 0.8 L and a respiratory rate of 12/min during resuscitation,[17] the ISO standard of < 5 cm H_2O results in a work of < 4.8 joules/min for a constant flow (such as might occur during inhalation), and a work of <

2.4 joules/min for a decelerating flow (such as might occur during exhalation).

The inspiratory resistance that we measured is an indicator of the effort required by the person squeezing the bag to direct flow to the patient. If this resistance is excessive, it can result in fatigue

Table 3. Pairs of Resuscitators with Significant Differences (p < 0.05) in Back Pressure, as Determined by Scheffe Analysis

Inspiratory Back Pressure
Intertech and SPUR
DMR and: SPUR, Hope 4
Mercury and: SPUR, Hope 4, Ambu, Laerdal, Hudson
Hospitak and: SPUR, Hope 4, Ambu, Laerdal, Respironics, Code Blue, Intertech, DMR, Mercury
Vitalograph and: SPUR, Hope 4, Ambu, Laerdal, Respironics, Code Blue, Intertech, DMR, Mercury

Expiratory Back Pressure
Hospitak and: Code Blue, Hudson, DMR, Hope 4, SPUR, Laerdal, Respironics, Ambu, Intertech, Mercury
Vitalograph and: Code Blue, Hudson, DMR, Hope 4, SPUR, Laerdal, Respironics, Ambu, Intertech, Mercury

Table 4. Pairs of Resuscitators with Significant Differences (p < 0.05) in Resistance, as Determined by Scheffe Analysis

Inspiratory Resistance
Hope 4 and SPUR
Ambu and SPUR
Laerdal and SPUR
Hudson and: SPUR, Hope 4, Ambu
Code Blue and: SPUR, Hope 4, Ambu
Respironics and: SPUR, Hope 4, Ambu
Intertech and: SPUR, Hope 4, Ambu, Laerdal, Hudson, Code Blue, Respironics
DMR and: SPUR, Hope 4, Ambu, Laerdal, Hudson, Code Blue, Respironics
Mercury and: SPUR, Hope 4, Ambu, Laerdal, Hudson, Code Blue, Respironics, Intertech, DMR
Hospitak and: SPUR, Hope 4, Ambu, Laerdal, Hudson, Code Blue, Respironics, Intertech, DMR, Mercury
Vitalograph and: SPUR, Hope 4, Ambu, Laerdal, Hudson, Code Blue, Respironics, Intertech, DMR, Mercury

Expiratory Resistance
Ambu and: DMR, Code Blue
Mercury and: DMR, Code Blue, Hudson, SPUR
Intertech and: DMR, Code Blue, Hudson, SPUR
Respironics and: DMR, Code Blue, Hudson, SPUR
Hope 4 and: DMR, Code Blue, Hudson, SPUR
Hospitak and: DMR, Code Blue, Hudson, SPUR, Laerdal, Ambu, Mercury, Intertech, Respironics, Hope 4
Vitalograph and: DMR, Code Blue, Hudson, SPUR, Laerdal, Ambu, Mercury, Intertech, Respironics, Hope 4

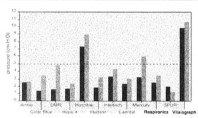

Fig. 2. Measured inspiratory ■ and expiratory ■ back pressures across 12 valves at flow of 50 L/min at which back pressure should be less than 5 cm H₂O.

for the person squeezing the bag. However, hand fatigue when using a manual resuscitator depends on other factors as well, including the compliance of the material used to construct the resuscitator bag, the endotracheal tube size, the resistance and compliance of the patient's lungs, and the minute ventilation. Because the inspiratory resistances that we measured were relatively low in most cases, these other factors might be more important causes of hand fatigue than the valve resistance.

The inspiratory resistance that we measured is also an indication of the effort required by a patient to spontaneously breathe through the resuscitator valve. However, the resistance to spontaneous inspiration is best evaluated by using a vacuum pump to draw a flow through the entire resuscitator and measuring the negative pressure generated at the outlet of the valve. This method evaluates the resistance to flow through the patient valve, the resuscitator bag, and the inlet valve of the resuscitator. Using this method, Mills et al[18] found that two resuscitators (Hospitak and Mercury) produced excessive resistive pressure to simulated spontaneous ventilation. Kissoon et al[19] recently reported their evaluation of the inspiratory and expiratory valve resistances of eight pediatric manual resuscitators. Although differences were found between the resistances of these pediatric resuscitator valves, all were considered acceptable by the authors.

Exhalation is usually passive. Expiratory resistance is the result of airway pathology (eg, bronchospasm, secretions) or imposed resistance (eg, endotracheal tubes, exhalation valves). When expiratory resistance is excessive, exhalation is prolonged. High expiratory resistance might prolong exhalation sufficiently to result in air-trapping (auto-PEEP). This is of particular concern when high expiratory resistance is coupled with short expiratory times, as might occur during rapid respiratory rates. Resuscitator valves with high resistance predispose the patient to acute airway pressure elevations and barotrauma during conditions of high expiratory flows. Conditions of high expiratory flow may be produced during a cough,[20,21] such as might occur during bag ventilation as part of airway suctioning. Intubated subjects can generate flows in excess of 250 L/min during a cough.[22]

An unexpected finding of this study was that resistance (inspiratory and expiratory) decreased in some resuscitators when flow increased (Table 2). In these resuscitators, an increase in flow presumably caused the valve to open farther, thus decreasing its resistance to flow. Although resuscitator valves have conventionally been classified as either "disc" or "duck-bill," the valves on many current-generation resuscitators do not easily fit into these categories. We thus did not attempt to evaluate the resistive properties of these resuscitators according to the design of the valve.

The decision to use a particular brand of resuscitator is based upon a number of considerations. Although we believe that one of those considerations should be the resistive properties of the valve, others include the ability of the resuscitator to deliver an adequate tidal volume and F_{IO_2}, the ease of use, and cost. Most manufacturers of resuscitators are continuously improving the design and performance of their products, and the resistive properties of some resuscitator valves may have improved since we collected the data for this study (Summer 1990). We believe that manufacturers should consider the resistive properties of their resuscitators and attempt to keep these resistances as low as possible. Given the generally low inspiratory and expiratory resistances that we found in this study, it would appear that resuscitator manufacturers are considering this in the design of their products. Although the resistances to inspiratory and expiratory flow were generally acceptable in this bench study, they were excessive for three resuscitators.

Additional work is needed in this area. The resistance to flow through the valves of pediatric resuscitators has only recently been reported,[19] and that of neonatal resuscitators should be evaluated and reported. It is also important to evaluate the resistance to flow through the valves of mouth-to-mask ventilation devices. Finally, the resistance to flow through the valves of resuscitators not considered in this study should be evaluated.

Conclusions

Significant differences were measured in the back pressures produced due to the flow resistance through the patient valves of the manual resuscitators evaluated in this study. Although the inspiratory and expiratory resistances found in this study were low in most cases, they may be considered excessive for the Hospitak and Vitalograph during both simulated inspiration and expiration and the Mercury during inspiration. Further work is needed to evaluate the clinical importance of these findings.

ACKNOWLEDGMENTS

We thank Matthew Vaughn for his assistance with data collection for this project.

PRODUCT SOURCES

Resuscitators:
CPR, Mercury Medical, Clearwater FL
Adult BagEasy with PEEP valve, Respironics,
Murrysville PA
Disposable Manual Resuscitator (DMR), Puritan-Bennett,
Lenexa KS
Hope 4, Matrx Medical, Orchard Park NY
Lifesaver Manual Resuscitator, Hudson RCI, Temecula CA
Code Blue, Vital Signs, Totowa NJ
Mark III, Ambu, Hanover MD
SPUR, Ambu, Hanover MD
Vitalograph, Vitalograph, Lenexa KS
Adult Resuscitator, Laerdal Medical, Armonk NY
Manual Pulmonary Resuscitator, Hospitak, Lindenhurst NY
Safe Response, Intertech Resources, Lincolnshire IL

Calibration Analyzer:
RT-200, Timeter, Lancaster PA

Flowmeter:
0-75, Timeter, Lancaster PA

Statistical Software:
SPSS/PC+, SPSS Inc, Chicago IL

REFERENCES

1. Hess D, Baran C. Ventilatory volumes using mouth-to-mouth, mouth-to-mask, and bag-valve-mask techniques. Am J Emerg Med 1985;3:292-296.
2. Elling R, Politis J. An evaluation of emergency medical technicians' ability to use manual ventilation devices. Ann Emerg Med 1983;12:765-768.
3. Harrison RR, Maull Kl, Keenan RL, Boyan CP. Mouth-to-mask ventilation: a superior method of rescue breathing. Ann Emerg Med 1982;11:74-76.
4. Johannigman JA, Branson RD, Davis K, Hurst JM. Techniques of emergency ventilation: a model to evaluate tidal volume, airway pressure, and gastric insufflation. J Trauma 1991;31:93-98.
5. Hess D, Goff G. The effects of two-hand versus one-hand ventilation on volumes delivered during bag-valve ventilation at various resistances and compliances. Respir Care 1987;32:1025-1028.
6. Hess D, Goff G, Johnson K. The effect of hand size, resuscitator brand, and use of two hands on volumes delivered during adult bag-valve ventilation. Respir Care 1989;34:805-810.
7. Jesudian MCS, Harrison R, Keenan RL, Maull KI. Bag-valve-mask ventilation—two rescuers are better than one: a preliminary report. Crit Care Med 1985;13:122-123.
8. Hess D, Spahr C. An evaluation of volumes delivered by selected adult disposable resuscitators: the effects of hand size, number of hands used, and use of disposable medical gloves. Respir Care 1990;35:800-805.
9. Barnes TA, Stockwell DL. Evaluation of ten manual resuscitators across an operational temperature range of −18°C to 50°C. Respir Care 1991;36:161-172.
10. Barnes TA, Potash R. Evaluation of five adult disposable operator-powered resuscitators. Respir Care 1989;34:254-261.
11. Barnes TA, McGarry WP. Evaluation of ten disposable manual resuscitators. Respir Care 1990;35:960-968.
12. International Standards Organization (ISO). Resuscitators intended for use with humans. Draft International Standard ISO/DIS 8382.
13. Marini JJ, Culver BH, Kirk W. Flow resistance of exhalation valves and positive end-expiratory pressure devices used in mechanical ventilation. Am Rev Respir Dis 1985;131:850-854.
14. Pinsky MR, Hrehocik D, Culpepper JA, Snyder JV. Flow resistance of expiratory positive-pressure systems. Chest 1988;94:788-791.
15. Wright PE, Marini JJ, Bernard GR. In-vitro versus in-vivo comparison of endotracheal tube airflow resistance. Am Rev Respir Dis 1989;140:10-19.
16. Sokal RR, Rohlf FJ. Introduction to biostatistics, 2nd ed. New York: WH Freeman & Co, 1987:27-45,185-510.
17. Healthcare provider's manual for basic cardiac life support. Dallas: American Heart Association, 1988.
18. Mills PJ, Baptiste J, Preston J, Barnas GM. Manual resuscitators and spontaneous ventilation—an evaluation. Crit Care Med 1991;19:1425-1431.
19. Kissoon N, Connors R, Tiffin N, Frewen TC. An evaluation of the physical and functional characteristics of resuscitators for use in pediatrics. Crit Care Med 1992;20:292-296.
20. Ulyatt DB, Judson JA, Trubuhovich RV, Galler LH. Cerebral arterial air embolism associated with coughing on a continuous positive airway pressure circuit. Crit Care Med 1991;19:985-987.
21. Banner MJ. Coughing may be hazardous to your health! Crit Care Med 1991;19:852-853.
22. Gal TJ. Effects of endotracheal intubation on normal cough performance. Anesthesiology 1980;52:324-329.

The Use of Preadmission Criteria To Predict Academic Success in a 4-Year Respiratory Care Curriculum

Timothy B Op't Holt EdD RRT and Crystal L Dunlevy EdD RRT

A number of studies have attempted to use objective and subjective criteria for allied health program admission to predict successful completion. We wanted to determine whether the criteria used in our program are valid predictors of academic success, to confirm the model on which our criteria are based, and to illustrate how this model may assist programs in complying with accreditation requirements. METHOD & SUBJECTS: The subject population was all students admitted from Spring 1982 through Spring 1988 (n = 79). Correlations and a multiple regression were performed between preprofessional grade point average (PPGPA), science-math GPA (S-M GPA), academic and interview points, and the GPA upon program completion (Exit GPA). RESULTS: The correlation between the PPGPA and Exit GPA was 0.76 and between the S-M GPA and Exit GPA 0.72. The regression equation was Exit GPA = 0.938 + 0.270 S-M GPA + 0.473 PPGPA. CONCLUSIONS: We conclude that the admissions criteria used in our program for the past 8 years are predictive and that the model previously described is valid, and we believe this model is appropriate for accreditation purposes. (Respir Care 1992;37:439-443.)

Introduction

A number of studies have attempted to evaluate the use of objective and subjective criteria before admission to predict the likelihood of successful completion of a program. The intent of these screening procedures is to assure that valuable and scarce resources are not squandered on the academically under-prepared student, especially if there are other qualified students waiting for admission. It is also interesting to note that some programs use no preadmission criteria; unfortunately, in the authors' experience, this leads only to an excessive attrition rate, poor morale, and fewer prepared graduates. In the present study we set out to determine whether the grade point average upon program completion (Exit GPA) could be predicted from preprofessional (PPGPA) and science-math GPA (S-M GPA).

The literature revealed that the use of the preprofessional grade point average has been regarded as the most reliable predictor of success and has been used both as an admission criterion and a predictor of program completion. In a study of admissions practices, Dietrich and Crowley[1] surveyed 11 different allied health professions and reported that 50-60% of programs weighed the PPGPA heavily, and that the science GPA was used concurrently in making admissions decisions. A number of studies have verified the importance of PPGPA and science GPA for predicting successful program completion. McGinnis studied students admitted to a physical therapy program who were successful in completing the program and determined that freshman-year GPA was the most predictive criterion, as the zero-order correlation with admission was 0.66.[2] Balogun et al[3] and Balogun alone[4] have reported that PPGPA accounted for 40% and

Dr Op't Holt and Dr Dunlevy are associated with the Respiratory Therapy Division, School of Allied Medical Professions, The Ohio State University, Columbus, Ohio.

A version of this paper was presented by Dr Op't Holt during the RESPIRATORY CARE OPEN FORUM at the 1991 AARC Annual Meeting held in Atlanta, Georgia.

38.5% of the variance in successful program completion. In a study of admissions practices in our program at The Ohio State University, Flanigan found that the science-math GPA and the English portion of the Scholastic Aptitude Test (SAT) or American College Test (ACT) were most predictive of successful completion.[5] She concluded that the S-M GPA could be used as the sole predictor. The weight of the S-M GPA was subsequently increased to 30% in admissions decisions. It was determined that a S-M GPA of 2.23 was necessary for 95% confidence that upon exit, the student would have at least the 2.20 GPA required for graduation. Based upon limited data points, students who have been admitted to the program with a S-M GPA below 2.23 have failed. No student enrolled with a S-M GPA at or above 2.23 has failed.

Assuming that no student could successfully complete a professional program starting with a PPGPA below a predetermined value, Posthuma and Noh[6] compared the success of 16 students admitted to occupational therapy programs based upon PPGPA alone and 16 students admitted based upon interview scores.[6] They reported no difference in the students' abilities to successfully complete the program. Therefore, once the minimum PPGPA had been met, it made no difference whether the students were interviewed (no other criteria needed to be considered).

Interviews have long been considered an important part of the admissions process. Although many consider interview results to be subjective, this process can provide an important opportunity to observe applicants firsthand. McGinnis[2] noted no correlation between interview scores and achievement. Schmalz et al[7] also noted the subjectivity of interviews and concluded that they do not reliably predict success.[7] Balogun et al[3] and Vargo et al[8] reported that interview scores were not predictive of academic success. Interviewing had been viewed by faculty at their institutions as a waste of valuable time, and the results of their studies led to discontinuation of the interview process. However, interview scores have correlated well in other studies with clinical performance. Balogun[4] found that interview scores accounted for 34.6% of the variation in clinical proficiency. Mazzoli,[9] in an abstract now 10 years old, also found that interview

scores correlated with clinical GPA. A candidate's knowledge of the profession can be determined by interview and assuring such knowledge was shown by Douce and Coates[10] to be an important factor in controlling attrition. Attrition due to lack of information or misinformation about the profession wastes both faculty and student time and money. Although interviews have been shown to be ineffective in predicting academic success, they are important in determining the potential for clinical skills and affective attributes.

Reference letters have lost their credibility due to the Family Educational Rights and Privacy Act (the Buckley amendment), which stipulates that students must be given the opportunity to inspect and review their own educational records and also stipulates that the institution must provide an opportunity for a hearing if a student wishes to challenge information therein.[11] Although it is improbable that a student would ask for a letter of reference from someone that he or she knows would not respond favorably, the stipulations of the Act probably discourage candor on a referee's part.

Another predictor of successful program completion may be the Allied Health Professions Admissions Test score (Schmalz et al,[7] Balogun et al,[3] and Balogun[4]). Balogun's studies showed that the Test added very little predictive strength ($< 8\%$) whereas PPGPA accounted for 40% of the variation in Exit GPA. Schmalz et al[7] found that the Otis Quick Scoring Mental Ability Test had some predictive ability. They also found that students transferring from 2-year institutions to 4-year institutions do not do as well as students transferring from other 4-year institutions, and this fact has been used as a method of applying weight to this criterion in admissions procedures. The student's age at application may also correlate positively with successful completion.

It is apparent from the literature that the PPGPA and the S-M GPA are the best predictive criteria for successful program completion. Interview scores seem to correlate with clinical abilities and allow determination of personal characteristics and an assessment of the applicant's knowledge of the field. However, this could also be done via a written statement. While numerous other objective and subjective criteria have been used in the admissions decisions, none correlate so strongly with academic success that they need to be included. We hypothesized that there are valid criteria for admissions predictive of successful program completion and that the most reliable criteria are PPGPA and S-M GPA. We also wanted to determine the lowest S-M GPA that would assure successful program completion, provided that the student's PPGPA was 2.2 or above.

Method and Subjects

All students who were admitted into the professional phase of the baccalaureate respiratory therapy program from Spring 1982 through Spring 1988 comprised the subject population (n = 79). All of these students subsequently graduated. Records indicate that the courses comprising the basis for the S-M GPA were consistent for this period (ie, single courses in biology, physics, and mathematics, and two courses in chemistry). Independent variables included the S-M GPA (based upon the courses listed), PPGPA (total), number of points scored on an interview (a structured interview form is used to evaluate pre-established nonacademic criteria related to knowledge of and commitment to the profession, goals, and personal attributes), the total number of points (based upon weighted GPAs and interview scores), and the points awarded for the PPGPA. The dependent variable was the Exit GPA (upon graduation). Correlations and a multiple regression were performed between the independent variables and the dependent variable, after the study by Flanigan.[5] Multiple regression was used because it is an appropriate method for studying the effects of several independent variables (in this instance, admission criteria) on one dependent variable, Exit GPA.[12] We used Minitab version 7.0 statistical software to calculate individual correlations between the independent variables and the dependent variable and for stepwise multiple regression.[13] Students with a cumulative GPA upon application of < 2.2 (on a 4-point scale), or a S-M GPA of < 2.0 (with two exceptions who were admitted on the strength of high PPGPAs) were not eligible for interview or consideration for admission because they were on academic probation. It is our policy to reconsider applicants who improve their GPA beyond these minimums.

Results

Correlations were calculated between the dependent variable (Exit GPA) and each of the independent variables, and are shown in Table 1. The independent variables with the highest correlations with Exit GPA were the S-M GPA (r = 0.72) and the PPGPA (r = 0.76).

Table 1. Simple Correlations (r) between Admissions Criteria and Exit GPA,* Obtained from 79 Students from Spring 1982 through Spring 1988

Admissions Criterion	r
Science-math GPA	0.72
Preprofessional GPA	0.76
Interview points	0.02
Total points	0.68
GPA points	0.78

*Grade point average on program completion.

Because the interview points, total points, and GPA points were derived from the S-M GPA and PPGPA values, point scores were not included in the multiple regression. The results of the regression between the S-M GPA, PPGPA, and the Exit GPA are shown in Table 2.

Table 2. Multiple Regression Analysis Showing the Relationship between S-M GPA,* PPGPA, and Exit GPA for 79 Students

Predictor Variable	Coefficient	Standard Error of Coefficient	t Ratio	p
S-M GPA	0.270	0.065	4.15	< 0.001
PPGPA	0.473	0.089	5.31	< 0.001

* S-M GPA = science-math grade point average.
PPGPA = preprofessional grade point average.
Exit GPA = grade point average on program completion.

The regression equation derived for the Exit GPA was Exit GPA = 0.938 + 0.270 S-M GPA + 0.473 PPGPA. The standard error of the estimate (SEE) was 0.196, and the adjusted R^2 was 0.643. Therefore, 64.3% of the variation in the Exit GPA may be explained by the use of the S-M GPA and the PPGPA. The correlation between Exit GPA and the linear combination of S-M GPA and PPGPA is 0.81.

Discussion

Based upon the correlations between the predictor variables and the dependent variable, only the PPGPA and the S-M GPA need be considered in the admissions decision to predict Exit GPA. The minimum PPGPA required to graduate from the Respiratory Therapy Division at The Ohio State University is 2.20. Therefore, the regression equation may be rearranged to determine the minimum S-M GPA required for admission. If we wish to be able to determine with 95% confidence that a given applicant will be successful in the program (an Exit GPA of at least 2.20), then the Exit GPA must be increased two standard errors of the estimate (SEEs) above the minimum Exit GPA, or to 2.59. Using this as the minimum Exit GPA, the equation to determine the minimum S-M GPA is

$$\text{S-M GPA} = \frac{\text{Exit GPA} - 0.473\,(\text{PPGPA}) - 0.938}{0.270}.$$

Substituting the derived Exit GPA of 2.59 into this equation, the minimum S-M GPA is 2.26. This confirms earlier work by Flanigan,[5] who determined that the minimum allowable S-M GPA is 2.23 to achieve a 2.68 Exit GPA, which was at the 95% confidence interval at the time of her study (1985). She also determined that the most reliable predictor was the S-M GPA. Based on these data, we may conclude that requiring at least a 2.2 PPGPA and 2.26 S-M GPA usually assures us that a student will successfully complete our respiratory therapy curriculum. This affirms Flanigan's report and challenges us to consider increasing the requisite S-M GPA to 2.26. Therefore, the Exit GPA can be predicted, with 95% confidence, when we have the PPGPA and S-M GPA.

The records of 8 students admitted with a S-M GPA of 1.75-2.21 were reviewed. When each student's S-M GPA and PPGPA were subjected to the regression equation, the strength of their PPGPA was sufficient to raise their Exit GPA to 2.66 or higher. There was no significant difference between the calculated Exit GPA and the actual Exit GPAs of these apparent outlier cases (p < 0.001).

The procedure described here could serve as a model for programs whose faculty wish to determine the minimum values of predictors that assure academic success. The predictors must be interval data, so that a correlation can be determined between each predictor and the Exit GPA. A regression is then performed between the Exit GPA and the predictors. The key is to determine the strength of only one predictor at a time. The other predictors would be those predetermined by the institution, such as institutional PPGPA or a test score (eg, ACT, SAT).

Another variable that we may wish to examine in the future is the interview score. Although the interview score correlated poorly with the Exit GPA, it may correlate well with clinical proficiency and/or positive affective evaluations, both of which are critical to becoming a successful respiratory care practitioner. At the present time, we painstakingly score the applicants' responses to interview questions. Whether we continue to do this in the light of these data or simply score the applicant's interview as satisfactory or unsatisfactory is yet to be determined.

This study also provides valid and reliable data that can be used to justify admission standards to the Joint Review Committee for Respiratory Therapy Education (JRCRTE). The guideline for Essential IV B states that "programs are encouraged to develop objective, success-related admission standards and/or prerequisites . . . ."[14] By completing a study such as this, any program faculty can determine the minimum values of success-related academic criteria required of its incoming students.

It is important to note that academic criteria alone may not always predict successful completion of the program because GPA (as at our institution) may not reflect psychomotor skill or affective attributes. Clinical courses are graded as Satisfactory or Unsatisfactory (S or U). A student receiving a clinical grade of Unsatisfactory cannot graduate until the course is repeated and a grade of Satisfactory is received.

One limitation of our study is that students who have a PPGPA < 2.20 are not interviewed or admitted; therefore, we cannot draw conclusions regarding their eventual academic or career outcome. In the event that enough persons with a PPGPA of ≥ 2.20 and a S-M GPA of 2.26 to fill a class did not apply, we would have less than 95% confidence that those students not fulfilling the criteria could successfully complete the program.

Conclusions

In conclusion, the admissions criteria used during the 7-year study period are predictive, in that no student has graduated who has not met the combination S-M GPA and PPGPA set by the program. We confirm the model constructed by Flanigan in 1985, and we believe that our model justifies the appropriateness of the admissions criteria to our program for the JRCRTE.

REFERENCES

1. Dietrich MC, Crowley JA. A national study of student selection practices in the allied health professions. J Allied Health 1982;11:248-260.
2. McGinnis ME. Admission predictors for pre-physical therapy majors. Phys Ther 1984;64(1):56-58.
3. Balogun JA, Karakoloff LA, Farina NT. Predictors of academic achievement in physical therapy. Phys Ther 1986;66(6):976-980.
4. Balogun JA. Predictors of academic and clinical performance in a baccalaureate physical therapy program. Phys Ther 1988;68(2):238-242.
5. Flanigan KS. A model for the evaluation of respiratory therapy program admissions criteria. Respir Care 1985; 30(5):334-338.
6. Posthuma B, Noh S. Interview scores and academic grades as selection criteria for admission to an occupational therapy program. Can J Occup Ther 1990;57(5): 285-291.
7. Schmalz GM, Rahr RR, Allen RM. The use of preadmission data to predict levels of success in selected allied health students. Occup Ther J Res 1990;10(6): 367-376.
8. Vargo JW, Madill HM, Davidson PR. The preadmission interview as a predictor of academic grades and fieldwork performance. Can J Occup Ther 1986;53 (4):211-215.
9. Mazzoli AJ. Predicting success in baccalaureate degree respiratory therapy programs (abstract). Respir Care 1982;27(10):1246.
10. Douce FH, Coates MA. Attrition in respiratory therapy education: causes and relationship to admissions criteria. Respir Care 1984;29(8):823-828.
11. Edwards HT, Nordin VD. Higher education and the law. Cambridge MA: Institute for Educational Management (Harvard University), 1979:751-761.
12. Kachigan SK. Multivariate statistical analysis. New York: Radius Press, 1982:180-189.
13. Minitab, Release 7.0. State College PA: Minitab Inc, 1989.
14. Joint Review Committee for Respiratory Therapy Education. Essentials and guidelines for an accredited educational program for the respiratory therapy technician and respiratory therapist. Euless TX: JRCRTE, 1986.

The Volume of Gas Emitted from Five Metered Dose Inhalers at Three Levels of Fullness

Dean Hess MEd RRT, Ann Daugherty BS RRT, and Mark Simmons MSEd RPFT RRT

We conducted this study to determine the volume of gas emitted from five commonly used metered dose inhalers (MDIs). MATERIALS & METHODS: We used the following MDIs: Alupent (Boehringer Ingelheim), Atrovent (Boehringer Ingelheim), Beclovent (Allen & Hanburys), Intal (Fisons), and Ventolin (Allen & Hanburys). The test system consisted of plastic bag, MDI adapter, 4-way stopcock, and 60-mL calibrated syringe. This system was glued together, and absence of leaks was confirmed by underwater testing. Each evaluation consisted of 10 puffs from the MDI into the bag, after which the volume in the bag was determined using the syringe, and the volume/puff was calculated by dividing by 10. Each MDI was evaluated at 3 levels of fullness: nearly full, partially empty, and nearly empty. Five measurements were made with each MDI brand, using a new MDI for each set of measurements. RESULTS: Although there was a significant difference in the volumes emitted between MDI ($p < 0.001$) and the levels of fullness ($p = 0.001$), the volume of gas emitted from these MDIs was small (≈15-20 mL). A significant interaction existed between MDI brand and level of fullness ($p = 0.001$). CONCLUSIONS: Based on prior studies of propellant toxicity coupled with our findings on the volumes of gas emitted from MDIs, we conclude that the volumes of gas emitted are too small to be clinically important in the care of adult patients. The volume of gas emitted from an MDI is only potentially important if MDIs are used with very small tidal volumes in a closed system (eg, infants). (Respir Care 1992;37:444-447.)

Metered dose inhalers (MDIs) are being used increasingly in both spontaneously breathing and mechanically ventilated patients. It is also becoming increasingly common to use MDIs at doses greater than the manufacturer-recommended dose in acutely ill patients.[1] In addition to active drug, the MDI contains chlorofluorocarbon (CFC) pro-

pellants. The vapor pressure of the CFC is high (300-500 kPa at 20°C). When the MDI is actuated, the contents of a small metering chamber within the inhaler are propelled out of the MDI by the CFC. The CFC becomes gas, leaving the drug suspended as micronized crystals. The volume of drug remaining after CFC vaporization has been estimated to be 25-100 μL, and to contain 50 μg-5 mg of drug.[2]

To our knowledge, very little work has been done to evaluate the total volume of drug and CFC propellant released from an MDI. Elliott et al[3] studied the effects of MDI propellants on respiratory gas monitors, and reported a volume of 15 mL from an albuterol (Proventil) MDI with each actuation. In a 1970 paper, Dollery et al[4] reported that a volume of 13 mL of gas was emitted from Alupent and Ventolin inhalers. In both of these studies, the volume of gas emitted from the MDI was a peripheral aspect of the study (ie, the study was not done

Mr Hess is Assistant Director, Department of Research, York Hospital, and Instructor, School of Respiratory Therapy; Ms Daugherty is Trauma Therapist, Pulmonary Services, York Hospital, and Clinical Instructor, School of Respiratory Therapy; Mr Simmons is Program Director, School of Respiratory Therapy—York Hospital and York College of Pennsylvania, York, Pennsylvania.

A version of this paper was presented by Mr Hess during the RESPIRATORY CARE OPEN FORUM at the 1991 AARC Annual Meeting held in Atlanta, Georgia.

Reprints: Dean Hess, Department of Research, York Hospital, 1001 South George St, York PA 17405.

specifically to determine the volume of gas emitted from the MDI). Other than these studies, we know of no reported evaluation of the volume emitted from the MDIs. We conducted this study to evaluate the volumes emitted from five commonly used MDIs.

Materials and Methods

The test system consisted of a plastic bag,* an MDI adapter, a 4-way stopcock, and a 60-mL calibrated syringe (Fig. 1). The system was glued together, and the absence of leaks was confirmed by underwater testing. Each evaluation consisted of 10 puffs from the MDI into the bag, after which the volume in the bag was determined using the syringe. The volume/puff was calculated by dividing the total volume by 10. The accuracy of the syringe was confirmed with a Timeter RT-200 Calibration Analyzer. All evaluations were made at a room temperature of 20°C.

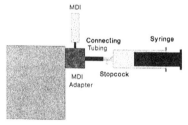

Fig. 1. Schematic diagram of test system used.

We evaluated five MDIs: Alupent, Atrovent, Beclovent, Intal, and Ventolin. We chose these MDIs because they are commonly used in our community and were the only ones available from our hospital formulary. Each type of MDI was evaluated at three levels of fullness: nearly full, partially empty, and nearly empty. The Intal MDI contains 112 puffs when full, and was evaluated at 1-10 puffs (nearly full, ≈102-112 puffs remaining in the MDI), 51-60 puffs (partially empty, ≈52-61 puffs remaining in the MDI), and 91-100 puffs (nearly

*Suppliers are identified in the Product Sources section at the end of the text.

empty, ≈12-21 puffs remaining in the MDI). The other MDIs each contain 200 puffs when full, and were evaluated at 1-10 puffs (nearly full, ≈191-200 puffs remaining in the MDI), 91-100 puffs (partially empty, ≈100-109 puffs remaining in the MDI), and 181-190 puffs (nearly empty, ≈10-19 puffs remaining in the MDI). The MDI was shaken before each activation, and 5 evaluations were made with each MDI brand (using a new MDI canister for each set of measurements).

Mean and standard deviation (SD) were calculated for each group of data. Two-way analysis of variance was performed using MDI brand as a grouping variable and volume remaining in the MDI (nearly full, partially empty, nearly empty) as a repeated measures factor. A computerized statistical analysis package was used, following appropriate statistical methodology.[5]

Results

The results are shown in Table 1 and Figure 2. There was a significant difference in the volumes emitted between MDI brands (p < 0.001) and levels of fullness (p < 0.001). There was a significant interaction effect between MDI brand and level of fullness (p = 0.001).

Table 1. Volumes Emitted from Five Metered Dose Inhalers (MDIs) at Three Levels of Fullness

| MDIs | Canister Condition | | |
	Nearly Full	Partially Empty	Nearly Empty
Alupent	15.6 (0.4)*	15.2 (0.01)	14.7 (0.2)
Atrovent	14.8 (0.2)	14.5 (0.1)	14.7 (0.2)
Beclovent	17.2 (0.3)	17.1 (0.3)	17.2 (0.2)
Intal	14.7 (0.3)	14.9 (0.2)	14.8 (0.3)
Ventolin	19.8 (0.4)	19.5 (0.4)	19.3 (0.3)

*Volumes are mean (SD) in mL.

Discussion

The results of this study indicate that the volumes of gas emitted from the 5 MDIs that we studied were small (≈15-20 mL), and are too small to be clinically important in the care of adult patients. Although the overall effect of MDI fullness was a

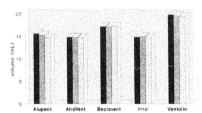

Fig. 2. Volumes of gas emitted from the MDIs evaluated at the three levels of fullness: ■ nearly full, ▨ partially empty, nearly empty.

decrease in volume emitted as the MDI became more nearly empty, there was a significant interaction effect between MDI brand and level of fullness. This means that the effect of fullness was not consistent among the MDI brands that we evaluated. As can be seen in Table 1 and Figure 2, level of fullness had little effect on the volumes emitted for Atrovent, Beclovent, and Intal. Although statistically significant, we do not believe that the differences in volume emitted between levels of fullness were clinically important (< 1 mL). The relatively small SDs reported in Table 1 also indicate that there was very little variability in the volumes emitted from the individual MDIs.

Elliott et al[3] evaluated the effects of bronchodilator-inhaler aerosol propellants on respiratory gas monitors. As part of that study, they added 1-12 MDI puffs of albuterol (Proventil, Schering Corp, Kenilworth NJ) to a sample bag to produce various concentrations of propellant. By measuring the dilution of oxygen in the bag, they determined that each MDI puff produced 15 mL of propellant gas, which agrees well with our results. They also found that the propellant produced artifactual readings with mass spectrometer systems, which may be clinically important when MDIs are used with intubated patients who are being monitored by mass spectrometry. Others have also reported erroneous mass spectrometer readings associated with the use of MDIs.[6,7]

It is important to recognize that we measured only the volumes of gas emitted per actuation from the MDIs. We did not measure the dose of active drug emitted, and the study was not designed to determine differences in doses of active drug. We also did not measure the exact number of puffs available from the MDIs. Differences in volumes emitted from the MDIs should *not* be interpreted to mean differences in dose of active drug, or differences in the number of puffs available from the MDIs.

The potential for toxicity associated with CFCs has been a concern for more than 20 years.[8] However, results of studies reported by Dollery et al[4,9] in the early 1970s suggested that CFC blood levels were relatively low, even with large doses from an MDI. In one study, volunteers inhaled 1 puff from an MDI every 10 minutes for 6 hours, with no progressive rise in blood concentration over that time, and no detection of CFC 2 hours following the last dose. In a patient with normal lungs who inhaled 3 puffs from an MDI, the highest concentration detected was 1.7 μg/mL. In a patient with obstructive lung disease who inhaled 6 puffs, the highest blood concentration of CFC was 0.63 μg/mL. Dollery et al[4] also reported that Ventolin and Alupent at that time (1970) used 50 μL of liquid fluorocarbon per dose, which resulted in 13 mL of gas emitted from the MDI. Although this data is now more than 20 years old, it agrees well with our finding of 15-20 mL of gas per puff from the 5 MDIs that we evaluated.

We did not evaluate the volumes emitted from all commercially available MDIs. Our objective was to evaluate those MDIs that are commonly used in our community. The 5 MDIs included in this study are those available in our hospital formulary. Persons interested in the volumes emitted from other MDIs (currently available or that may become available in the future) could use our methodology to determine such. Our data suggest that the volumes emitted from MDIs may vary little between MDIs.

We believe that the volume of gas emitted from an MDI is too small to be important in most clinical conditions. Although the use of greater numbers of puffs from an MDI has become more common, there is typically only one puff provided per breath and a minute or longer elapses between puffs. The volume of gas emitted from an MDI may be potentially important if MDIs are used with very small tidal volumes in a closed system. Use of an MDI with small tidal volumes in a closed system could result in an increased pressure and a decreased oxygen concentration, but additional data are needed to determine whether there are any clinically important consequences related to this. MDIs have been used safely and effectively in conjunction with auxiliary spacer devices in children[10,11] and infants as young as 1.6 months of age.[12-14] When an auxiliary spacer device is used, the volume from an MDI is relatively small in comparison to the volume in the auxiliary device. To our knowledge, the use of MDIs with intubated mechanically ventilated infants has not been reported. Further work is needed to determine the clinical circumstances, if any, in which the volume of gas emitted from an MDI might be important.

Conclusions

Based on prior studies of propellant toxicity[4,9] and our findings on the volumes of gas emitted from MDIs, we conclude that the volumes are too small to be of concern in most clinical circumstances. Although there are small differences in the volumes emitted from MDIs between brands and levels of fullness, these are not clinically important.

PRODUCT SOURCES

Metered Dose Inhalers:
Ventolin (albuterol), Allen & Hanburys, Division of Glaxo, Research Triangle Park NC
Intal (cromolyn sodium), Fisons Pharmaceuticals, Rochester NY
Beclovent (beclomethasone dipropionate), Allen & Hanburys, Division of Glaxo, Research Triangle Park NC
Atrovent (ipratropium bromide), Boehringer Ingelheim Pharmaceuticals, Richfield CT
Alupent (metaproterenol sulfate), Boehringer Ingelheim Pharmaceuticals, Richfield CT

MDI Adapter:
RTC 23-D, Instrumentation Industries, Bethel Park PA

Glue:
Household cement, Duro, Loctite Corp, Cleveland OH

Pleated Storage Bag:
Ziploc (half gallon size), Dow Consumer Products, Indianapolis IN

Syringe and Stopcock:
Becton Dickinson, Rutherford NJ

Calibration Analyzer:
RT-200, Timeter Instrument Corp, Lancaster PA

Statistical Software:
SPSS/PC+, SPSS Inc, Chicago IL

REFERENCES

1. MacIntyre NR, Brougher P, Hess D, Newhouse MT, Pierson DJ, Ziment I, and consensus conference committee. American Association for Respiratory Care: aerosol consensus statement—1991. Respir Care 1991;36: 916-921.
2. Newman SP. Aerosol generators and delivery systems. Respir Care 1991;36:939-951.
3. Elliott WR, Raemer DB, Goldman DB, Philip JH. The effect of bronchodilator inhaler aerosol propellants on respiratory gas monitors. J Clin Monit 1991;7:175-180.
4. Dollery CT, Draffan GH, Davies DS, Williams FM, Conolly ME. Blood concentrations in man of fluorinated hydrocarbons after inhalation of pressurized aerosols. Lancet 1970;2:1164-1166.
5. Sokal RR, Rohlf FJ. Biostatistics, 2nd ed. New York: WH Freeman & Co, 1987:27-45,185-210.
6. Kharasch ED, Sivarajan M. Aerosol propellant interference with clinical mass spectrometers. J Clin Monit 1991;7:172-174.
7. Gravenstein N, Theisen GJ, Knudsen AK. Misleading mass spectrometer reading caused by an aerosol propellant. Anesthesiology 1985;63:70-72.
8. Taylor GJ, Harris WS. Cardiac toxicity of aerosol propellants. JAMA 1970;214:81-85.
9. Dollery CT, Williams FM, Draffan GH, Wise G, Sahyoun H, Paterson JW, et al. Arterial blood levels of fluorocarbons in asthmatic patients following use of pressurized aerosols. Clin Pharmacol Ther 1974;15:59-66.
10. Sly RM, Barbera JM, Middleton HB, Eby DM. Delivery of albuterol aerosol by Aerochamber to young children. Ann Allergy 1988;60:403-406.
11. Benton G, Thomas RC, Nickerson BG, McQuitty JC, Okikawa J. Experience with a metered-dose inhaler with a spacer in the pediatric emergency department. AJDC 1989;143:678-681.
12. Mallol J, Barrueto L, Girardi G, Toro O. Bronchodilator effect of fenoterol and ipratropium bromide in infants with acute wheezing: use of MDI with a spacer device. Pediatr Pulmonol 1987;3:352-356.
13. Kraemer R, Frey U, Sommer CW, Russi E. Short-term effect of albuterol, delivered via a new auxiliary device, in wheezy infants. Am Rev Respir Dis 1991;144:347-351.
14. Conner WT, Dolovich MB, Frame RA, Newhouse MT. Reliable salbutamol administration in 6- to 36-month-old children by means of a metered dose inhaler and Aerochamber with mask. Pediatr Pulmonol 1989;6:263-267.

Points of View

Patient-Focused Hospitals: An Opportunity for Respiratory Care Practitioners

Gregory M Snyder BS RRT

Introduction

A new concept in hospital structure, the patient-focused hospital (PFH), is evolving in America.[1] The PFH concept brings respiratory care practitioners (RCPs) an unsurpassed opportunity to increase the breadth and depth of clinical care we provide and to grow in professional stature.

The PFH concept was developed by the Booz, Allen & Hamilton consulting firm for the purposes of improving services and cutting costs.[1] However, improved service and savings will occur not by layoffs and working harder but by redesigning hospital infrastructure. Successful companies around the world are re-engineering their processes to become more efficient;[2] hospitals and the professionals who staff them can do the same.[3]

The political and economic spotlight is focusing ever more sharply on hospitals. Patients wonder why they have to wait hours for routine care and why care costs so much. My department has been specifically questioned by patients asking why oxygen costs $40 per day and why a medicated nebulizer treatment costs $24.* Many of the answers to these questions lie in the inherently inefficient structure of hospitals. Today's hospital structure encourages overspecialization, services located all over the hospital, and documentation in quadruplicate.[1] The PFH concept offers RCPs, who are by tradition innovators, an opportunity to improve clinical care and grow in professional stature.

The cornerstone of the PFH concept is the implementation of five operating principles:

- Broaden skills of providers.
- Move services closer to the patient.
- Simplify processes.
- Streamline paperwork and eliminate duplication.
- Focus patient populations.

Implementation of Operating Principles

Broaden Skills

The PFH concept requires the presence of clinicians who will possess a far broader array of clinical skills than the clinicians of today. Respiratory therapists will provide the services listed in the AARC Uniform Reporting Manual[4] and new ones as well. In our hospital we are training therapists to start intravenous lines (I.V.s), attach electrodes and record electrocardiograms, perform basic laboratory tests, and perform phlebotomy. It seems logical that a therapist already skilled in drawing arterial samples for blood gas analysis could perform phlebotomy and start an I.V. In the neonatal unit, respiratory therapists are being trained to make patient assessments and provide nursing care.

The broadly skilled clinician concept extends to other disciplines also. Nurses,[5] radiology technicians,[6] and clinical laboratory technicians[7] are all broadening their professional reach. Our hospital will teach nurses to provide basic respiratory care such as nebulizer treatments, incentive spirometry (IS), chest physical therapy (CPT), and oxygen administration. Figures 1 and 2 illustrate how respiratory care and nursing can share delivery of many services that are now considered the sole dominion of one discipline. In our institution, we plan to teach this same range of basic respiratory skills to other clinicians as we move forward with the patient-focus concept. The basis of our cross-

---

*Current price at Sentara Norfolk General Hospital. During May 1991, we made a regional survey that suggests approximate equivalency at other hospitals, unpublished data.

training will be the AARC Clinical Practice Guidelines.[8]

Selected RC tasks now
(many exclusionary tasks, little oVerlap)

Selected nursing tasks now
(many exclusionary tasks, little oVerlap)

Fig. 1. Venn diagram illustrating selected respiratory therapy and nursing tasks in current hospital structure. Very little overlap exists in tasks performed by different disciplines.

It is important to understand that not all services will be shared. The trend is for each discipline to retain the most complex 20-40% of services while sharing the more basic 60-80% of skills. Many clinicians from other disciplines can be taught to provide and evaluate the results of low-flow oxygen therapy, IS, CPT, and nebulized medications. For example, the time required to learn to manage a ventilator makes it economically infeasible to train everyone to do so.

Selected RC tasks in PFH
(few exclusionary tasks, lots of oVerlap)

Selected nursing tasks in PFH
(few exclusionary tasks, lots of oVerlap)

Fig. 2. Venn diagram projecting selected respiratory therapy and nursing tasks in the patient-focused hospital environment. There will be much overlap in the tasks of different disciplines. The same concept can be applied to respiratory/radiology, respiratory/physical therapy, respiratory/medical technology, or other fields.

Shared services will also serve as a source of job enrichment. Just as we teach others to provide basic respiratory procedures, RCPs will have the opportunity to provide more comprehensive care by taking vital signs, starting I.V.s, dispensing medications, and other routine services. Since diversity of tasks correlates positively with job satisfaction,[9] recruiting and retention of RCPs in the PFH environment should improve.

Currently our hospital provides nearly all cross-training in-house. To assure competency, we are developing in-depth educational forums, recertification programs, and continuous quality improvement. However, the multicompetent provider is already being trained at several visionary schools. At Southern Illinois University, School of Technical Careers, respiratory therapy students can minor in medical technology or radiology technology.[10]

Move Services Closer to the Patient

Moving services closer to the patient means having 80% of the personnel, equipment, and supplies located at the bedside or in the confines of the operating center. The majority of respiratory therapists, pharmacists, physical therapists, radiology technicians, and phlebotomists will be based in operating centers rather than in centrally based departments. For example, to move respiratory services closer to the emergency room (ER) patients, we will assign staff therapists to the ER. Currently we deliver a 'stat' ER nebulizer treatment within 5 minutes of receiving the order. We think this is efficient; however, if a patient is in the throes of status asthmaticus, 5 minutes seems like an eternity. We are planning to designate one therapist to be in the ER continuously. When not providing respiratory care, he will start I.V.s, give medications, perform phlebotomy, and perform laboratory tests. We will provide nebulizer treatments within 60 seconds of receiving the order. If the RCP is caring for another patient, the cross-trained nurse, laboratory technician, or pharmacist will administer the treatment.

Equipment will also move to the operating centers. Each operating center will contain ventilators, monitors, and laboratory equipment. Each operating center will contain enough laboratory equipment to run all routine tests such as blood gases, electrolytes, hemoglobin and hematocrit, blood sugar, and urinalysis. Minor repairs and preventive maintenance will be performed in the operating center; major repairs will go to clinical engineering. Moving services closer to the patient means equipment redundancy and costly startup. (We estimate doubling capital expenditures in our institution.) However, the theory is that people time is valuable, machine time is cheap. By saving people time, we will save overall. Because implementation of the PFH concept will occur in stages, startup costs can be spread over time. Once all equipment is in place, we should be able to provide faster and less expensive service.

Simplify Processes

Hospitals are recognized as one of the most complex management environments extant.[11] The complexity of tasks, the regulatory environment, the litigious environment, the hundreds of job descriptions, the professional level of performance required for even basic tasks, and the process orientation of patient care all contribute to a tremendous management challenge. In his paper "Real Work," Zaleznik points out that in most companies process and politics get more attention than real work.[12]

A key feature of the PFH model is to simplify processes and thereby eliminate unnecessary work—freeing up time that is better spent on our real job, patient care. As personnel acquire broader skills and as services are moved closer to the patient, there will be many opportunities to simplify our processes. Figure 3 depicts the simplified process for ordering nebulized bronchodilator in the PFH environment. Three steps are saved. If one multiplies this small savings by millions of events, one can eliminate a tremendous amount of unnecessary work.

Streamline Paperwork and Eliminate Duplication

Now it is common, even routine, for a patient chart to contain the same information duplicated time and time again. Blood gases are a good example. Blood gas results can nearly always be found on ventilator flow sheets, in the respiratory therapy notes, in the nursing notes, in the physician notes, and on the laboratory slips. Think how often this scenario repeats itself with blood gases, laboratory values, and physical findings on every patient! As RCPs become unit-based rather than central-department based, communication among RCPs and other providers will improve. As clinicians, we will be able to put less in writing and speak, person-to-person, more. Much of our unnecessary documentation can be eliminated.

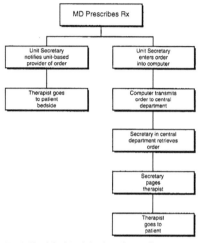

Fig. 3. The left side of the flow diagram illustrates the steps that will be required for a patient to receive a nebulizer treatment in the patient-focused hospital environment. The right side of the flow diagram illustrates the steps necessary in the current structure.

Charting by exception is another option that will eliminate duplication of paperwork. As the name implies, charting by exception documents only those findings that vary from previously established norms.[13] Here is an example. For years therapists in our hospital have charted pre-treatment, treatment, and post-treatment pulse rates when giving bronchodilators. In the new environment, we will chart only when the pulse varies from established standards of practice as spelled out by protocol. Developing the necessary workable protocols takes time and money upfront but will pay off in time saved over the long run.

Focus Patient Populations

To the extent feasible, patients will be grouped according to major categories of illness. This is probably the least innovative concept in the PFH ideal. Hospitals have tried for decades to group patients by disease. Sometimes we succeed, other times we fail. Human beings, and their illnesses, are too varied to allow 'neat' categorization. Nevertheless, grouping patients in this fashion is something we need to do as much as possible. When clinicians see the same type of illness over and over, they naturally become more adept at dealing with that particular illness. Our hospital has defined seven operating centers, and all patients will be admitted to one of the centers: Cardiac, Surgery, Oncology, Ambulatory, Women's Health, MPR (Medicine, Psych, and Renal), and TRON (Trauma, Rehab, Ortho, and Neuro). Patients requiring intensive respiratory care will be found in nearly all operating centers. Consequently, each center will have its own team of RCPs.

Issues Affecting Implementation

During the implementation of the PFH concept in our department, several issues have arisen repeatedly, and these or similar issues will almost certainly affect other hospitals embarking on the PFH concept and must be effectively resolved.

Fear of Having To "Work Harder"

The old adage "work smarter, not harder" could have been written for the PFH scenario. The past decade of diagnosis-related groups (DRGs), budget cuts, and doing more with less have left many RCPs intensely skeptical of any management efforts to cut costs. It is important to realize just how sweeping the changes in a PFH hospital will be. Imagine how much time will be saved if blood gas results are noted only once or twice compared to the current entry system. How much time will be saved when nebulizer treatments can be started with only three steps? These are the areas in which PFH will help—by eliminating the seemingly ceaseless documentation and interdepartmental communication.

Fear of Losing Professional Identity

Upon first learning of the PFH, many RCPs (and this writer was included) fear that they will lose their professional identity, they will "work for a nurse" and "have to do bedpans."

Some RCPs believe that as central departments delegate most of the day-to-day operations to unit-based managers, the central department's authority or prestige may diminish. In some respects this will be true and in other respects false. Central departments will be much smaller, but will retain the key functions of education, clinical standards, continuous quality improvement, and administration of JCAHO requirements. The conflict between central and dispersed control is classic; but with modern databases and communication, hospitals can enjoy the benefits of both systems.[2] As central departments share functions with unit-based services, management will change also. It is likely that a good respiratory manager will supervise nurses, radiology technicians, physical therapists, and laboratory technicians. Clinical managers will be selected on the basis of their managerial competence, not their profession.

In the PFH environment, the respiratory therapist will perform a greater variety of clinical tasks than he or she currently performs. We will also retain control over the top 20-40% of our clinical skills. No hospital management in its right mind would suggest that someone other than a respiratory therapist manage ventilators unless that someone had extensive training in ventilator management. Although almost anyone can learn to turn the knobs of a ventilator, it takes time and practice to learn to evaluate the results of that knob turning. From clinicians, to middle managers, to hospital CEOs, each person must be acutely aware of the capabilities and limitations of providers. We will still need the services that only highly trained specialists can provide. One mistake can bring death to the ventilator-dependent patient.

On a more mundane level, few clinicians find bedpan duty exciting. Yet, while it is possible that any clinician may on occasion have bedpan duty, many routine activities will be handled by patient aides. And, regardless of who provides the bedpan, be assured that there are few tasks for which a patient will express a greater gratitude than having this task performed quickly and skillfully!

Fear of Layoffs

The PFH hospital will do less unnecessary work as discussed above, and that may translate into fewer jobs. However, implementing PFH is by necessity an incremental process that may take 5-7 years in a large hospital. Any net decrease in staffing can be handled by attrition. And there is no certainty that there will be a net loss of jobs. I believe that ever-increasing medical technology, and an aging population, will increase the need for broadly skilled providers.

Higher Pay Expectations of the Multiskilled Individual

As hospitals move toward a patient-focused environment, competitive forces may drive clinical salaries higher. As existing staff acquire more skill and responsibility, they will expect more pay—and rightfully so. Our job as managers and clinicians will be to ensure that the PFH model removes structural impediments, provides outcome-oriented work, improves the work environment, and pays competitive salaries. If the pay and work expectations of the multiskilled RCP are not met, the RCP will migrate to a competing hospital after having been trained at the earlier institution's expense!

Challenge to Educators To Train Multiskilled Individuals

In order for the patient focused environment to have broad acceptance and sucess, formal education must also change. Although a few farsighted college-based programs exist for training multicompetent individuals, most programs still are designed to train a specific specalist—a respiratory therapist, a nurse, or a radiologic technician. The successful education programs of the future will train people in a variety of skills. Multicompetent individuals will find better and higher paying jobs than their specialized counterparts. Furthermore, and perhaps most important to the sucess of the PFH concept, hospital administrators view multicompetent individuals as an advantage to the hospital.[14]

In-house educators face challenges as well. Professionals are notoriously difficult to educate.[15] Cross-training will occur for credentialed staff at many levels of clinical knowledge, and, as a consequence, educational programs must meet the needs of both neophyte clinicians and advanced professionals. Furthermore, each class or topic will have to be taught dozens of times. And, finally, the cross-training itself must be cost-effective and yet comprehensive. The surest way of 'torpedoing'

PFH efforts would be to skimp on teaching efforts and learning time.

Concerns that Quality of Care May Deteriorate

This concern is particularly pervasive among the most motivated and professional RCPs—and rightfully so! If we fail to provide quality care, we may as well not provide care at all. Concern over the loss of quality stems from the fact that what we know, as individual RCPs, was acquired through a long period of academic application, successful completion of national exams, and dedicated practice; for that reason, it is reasonable to fear that care may deteriorate if shared with professionals from other disciplines. What appears simple to the uninitiated can be quite complex; in the same way that a virtuoso makes playing an instrument look simple, a skilled RCP makes performing an intubation or an arterial puncture or adjusting a ventilator to minimize patient-ventilator asynchrony appear easy. But, they are not. These skills were acquired only through study and diligent practice—and, yes, mistakes.

The way to deal with this concern is through education. Any hospital embarking on the PFH concept must be willing and have the resources to spend enormous amounts of money on education. (At our institution, we estimate 160 hours of training at an average wage of $14/hour for a total of $2,240/employee.) It is also important to conceptualize what tasks will be shared with what disciplines. Nurses, radiology technicians, physical therapists, and other providers should be taught only those respiratory tasks that they will perform frequently and can learn fairly quickly.

Quality of care must be reviewed continuously and re-teaching must occur when indicated. Continuous Quality Improvement (CQI) will be a key function of central departments. Failure to provide CQI will lead to inevitable dilution and degradation of skills, respiratory complications if therapy is poorly performed, and less money for wages, capital improvement, and re-investment.

Unrealistic Management Expectations

As the PFH concept becomes more widely known, some management teams may focus on the advantages of such a system and ignore or minimize the complexity and costs associated with changing from a traditional hospital to a PFH. Management teams may try, with insufficient planning and understanding, to rush headlong into a PFH environment. Such precipitous moves will surely fail because they ignore significant clinical and managerial issues.

The path to a patient-focused environment will be long and rocky. The PFH concept is good, but that alone does not guarantee success. Institutions implementing PFH have spent months or years just on the planning process.[1] Because there are few multiskilled providers, hospitals must bear the cost of thousands of hours of time spent on education. Operating budgets will look worse, not better, for an extended period of time. There will be turf battles, state licensure issues, revised job descriptions, and perhaps increased union activity. Intense and rapid change is always traumatic,[16] and educating a staff that will frequently have valid and deep concerns takes time, energy, and money.

I believe that in our current dynamic environment it is essential that respiratory managers and clinicians take a proactive role in the implementation of PFH. The issues raised in this article can provide you with the benefit of our experience.

In Conclusion

It is this writer's firm belief that the clinically and financially successful hospitals of the next generation will employ the patient-focused model. American hospitals are where the American auto industry was 30 years ago—on the verge of a long descent into financial failure. I do not envision that we will see Hospitals by Honda or Toyota; but I do believe that if we fail to repair our shortcomings ourselves, the government will attempt to repair them for us. And, I believe that government intervention will lead to rationing, higher taxes, and a much lower level of care than currently provided.

The transition to a patient-focused environment will be arduous. There will be fear, uncertainty, and criticism along the way. However, I believe the PFH model is the best option for health-care reform extant. Fifty years ago we were known as oxygen delivery technicians. We founded a professional

organization and were called inhalational therapists. Our role expanded and we became respiratory therapists. Now we are respiratory care practitioners, and we have the finest professional organization of all allied health fields.

RCPs are traditionally innovators. Now we have an opportunity to rename, and thus redefine, ourselves and our profession. I encourage respiratory care practitioners to seize the opportunity provided by the PFH concept. We can, and should, learn more job skills. There should be a national move to our becoming cardiopulmonary practitioners rather than respiratory care practitioners. We should de-emphasize 1-year technician programs and emphasize 2-year programs—a suggestion roughly similar to the recommendation of the AARC Delphi study.[17] Indeed, a former chairman of the Board of Medical Advisors (BOMA), Dr William F Miller, has been quoted as saying that even 2-year programs are inadequate and that we should train RCPs in 4-year programs![18] The practitioner who can manage ventilators, perform EKGs, measure hemodynamics, intubate, start I.V.s, give medications, and take x-rays will be far more valuable than the practitioner with fewer skills.

All respiratory managers and clinicians should familiarize themselves with the PFH concept. Read the literature, go to seminars, and make site visits. Many PFH concepts are already practiced—especially in smaller hospitals. Focus on the five key elements of the PFH concept. Learn all you can and then decide how you can help our profession grow into its next stage of development.

ACKNOWLEDGMENTS

I thank Tim Sharkey BS RRT of the Children's Hospital of the King's Daughters in Norfolk for his help with preparing figures and legends.

REFERENCES

1. Lathrop P. The patient-focused hospital. Healthcare Forum J 1991;July/August:17-23.
2. Hammer M. Reengineering work: don't automate, obliterate. Harvard Business Review 1990;68July/August: 104-112.
3. Eubanks P, Hagland M, Grayson M, Sabatino F. Restructuring care: patient focus is key to innovation. Hospitals 1991;65(August 5):26-33.

4. Giordano S, Anderson H, Boroch M, Jones W, Kacmarek R, Ritz R, et al. AARC uniform reporting manual, 3rd edition. Dallas TX: American Association for Respiratory Care, 1989.
5. Hast A, Serish A. Cross-training in critical care. Critical Care Nurse 1990;6:74-79.
6. Trovato G. The future radiologic technologist (editorial). Applied Radiology 1987;June:7.
7. Starrs C. The multi-skilled movement: a new wave for clinical laboratory science. Clinical Laboratory Science 1989;2(Jul/Aug):204-210.
8. American Association for Respiratory Care, Clinical Practice Guidelines Steering Committee. The AARC clinical practice guidelines. Respiratory Care 1991;36:1398-1426.
9. Hmelo C, Axton K. Job satisfaction and task complexity among respiratory care practitioners. Respir Care 1989;34:1129-1134.
10. Beachey W. Multicompetency education in allied health: a trend of the future? AARC Times 1986;10(5):47.
11. Flower J. It's Late in the day: a conversation with Peter Drucker. Part 2. Healthcare Forum J 1991;May/June:33-41.
12. Zaleznik A. Real work. Harvard Business Review 1989;67(Jan-Feb):57-64.
13. Burke L, Murphy J. Charting by exception: a cost-effective, quality approach. New York: John Wiley & Sons, 1982.
14. Beachey W. Multicompetency needs in respiratory care: results of survey of respiratory therapy alumni and hospital administrators. Respir Care 1988;33:348-353.
15. Argyris C. Teaching smart people how to learn. Harvard Business Review 1991;69(May-June):99-109.
16. Scott C, Jaffee D. From crises to culture change. Healthcare Forum J 1991;May/June:33-41.
17. O'Daniel C, Cullen D, Douce H, Ellis G, Mikles S, Wiezalis C, et al. The future educational needs of RCPs: a Delphi study. Respir Care 1992;37:65-78.
18. Bunch D. Pioneers in respiratory care: William F Miller MD. AARC Times 1989;13(7):17-26.

Circle 112 on reader service card

Nicotine Use Can Lead to Dependence.
Learn About It and Its Treatment

"Nicotine Dependency Evaluation and Treatment" is an Individual Independent Study Package (IISP) to help you understand the physiologic effects of nicotine, tests, and questions used to evaluate dependency.

It will give you an understanding of nicotine and how it affects the chemistry of the brain, how it can be measured in bodily fluids, and the value of using self-tests to determine addiction levels. This IISP also teaches the importance of nicotine replacement and how it can be enhanced with behavioral counseling.
Item SC1, $10 (60 pages)

Prepare Yourself for the Role of Smoking Cessation Counselor

"Bedside Counseling of the Hospitalized Smoker" is an Individual Independent Study Package to prepare you for the role of smoking cessation counselor to hospital inpatients. Hospitalization presents a unique opportunity to assist patients to quit smoking.

This IISP helps you understand the role of the bedside nicotine-dependence counselor and how to assess the inpatient smoker. You will be able to help patients cope with nicotine withdrawal, increase motivation for permanent cessation, and be able to understand factors contributing to smoking relapse.
Item SC2, $10 (80 pages)

- -

Please send me:

■ Nicotine Dependency Evaluation and Treatment (SC1)
■ Bedside Counseling of the Hospitalized Smoker (SC2)

$10 each, shipping $2, 25¢ each additional item.

Payment enclosed in the amount of $_____

Bill to P.O. Number _____

Charge to my ■ MasterCard ■ Visa. Expiration Date _____

Card Number_____

Signature_____

Ship to Attn:_____

Bill to Attn: _____

Institution_____

Address _____

City/State/Zip_____

American Association for Respiratory Care • 11030 Ables Lane • Dallas, TX 75229
Telephone (214) 243-2272 • FAX (214) 484-6010

Test Your Radiologic Skill

Charles G Durbin Jr MD and
Douglas B Eden BS RRT, Section Editors

Stumped in the ICU

Scott E Copeman RRT

A 71-year-old man with a history of heavy cigarette smoking, alcohol abuse, chronic obstructive pulmonary disease, hypertension, non-insulin-dependent diabetes mellitus, and prostate cancer was referred to our hospital, presenting with dyspnea on exertion and hemoptysis. Pulmonary function tests were abnormal with a forced expiratory volume in one second (FEV_1) of 1.94 showing moderate airway obstruction, with a decreased diffusing capacity. Saturation of arterial oxygen (S_{aO_2}) was normal at rest, but decreased with exercise. This was consistent with his history of emphysema. Bronchoscopy was performed, and the trachea and left bronchial tree were found to be normal. However, the orifice of the right bronchus intermedius was found to be nearly completely obstructed. Bronchial biopsies revealed metastatic Grade III squamous cell carcinoma. After outpatient metastatic workup, including further tests that revealed no extrathoracic disease, the patient underwent right thoracotomy with pneumonectomy. At surgery, a large 5- to 6-cm mass was found in the hilus of the right lung. The mass extended down into the subcarinal area and into the pulmonary veins. The lymph nodes contained squamous cell carcinomas. The bronchial stump was found to be free of tumor and was closed in the normal manner and tested to be leak free at 50 cm H_2O [4.903 kPa].

The immediate postoperative course was unremarkable, with the patient extubated in the recovery room and placed on F_{IO_2} (fraction of inspired oxygen) 0.40 by close-fitting mask. He was transferred to the surgical intensive care unit for invasive hemodynamic monitoring by Swan-Ganz catheter. An arterial line was placed for continued blood pressure monitoring and as a sampling site for blood gas determination.

Mr Copeman is a staff therapist at the Mayo Clinic, Rochester, Minnesota.

On the second postoperative day, the patient developed acute dyspnea and tachypnea and was found to be hypoxemic. He was subsequently electively intubated and placed on mechanical ventilation with F_{IO_2} 0.70, Assist/Control of 12, tidal volume 0.650 L with 5 cm H_2O [0.490 kPa] positive end-expiratory pressure (PEEP). A chest roentgenogram was ordered to confirm endotracheal tube placement (Fig. 1). His oxygenation improved steadily. Ventilator settings were reduced to synchronized intermittent mandatory ventilation and pressure support with an F_{IO_2} 0.40.

Fig. 1. Anteroposterior chest radiograph of a 71-year-old man, taken 2 days following a thoracotomy.

The patient proved to be very difficult to wean, however, and on the morning of the 6th postoperative day, a change was noted on the routine morning chest roentgenogram (Fig. 2). Ventilator PEEP was subsequently set at 0. Arterial blood gases were found adequate on an F_{IO_2} of 0.40. Subsequently, the patient developed increasing respiratory distress, and blood gases revealed hypoxemia with a P_{aO_2} (partial pressure of arterial oxygen) of 54 torr [7.198 kPa]. F_{IO_2} was increased to 1.0 and a 'stat' chest roentgenogram was ordered (Fig. 3).

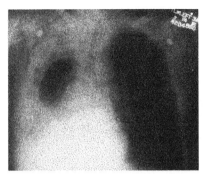

Fig. 2. Anteroposterior chest radiograph of the subject in Fig. 1, taken on Postoperative Day 6.

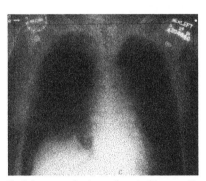

Fig. 3. Anteroposterior chest radiograph of the same 71-year-old man in Figures 1 & 2 after he began to experience hypoxemia and respiratory distress.

Questions

Radiographic Findings on Postoperative Day 2:
What does the chest radiograph in Figure 1 show?
Radiographic Findings on Postoperative Day 6:
What do the chest radiographs in Figures 2 & 3 show?

**Answers and Discussion
on Next Page**

Answers and Discussion

Radiographic Findings: The chest radiograph in Figure 1 shows an endotracheal tube (ETT) and a nasogastric tube in place, with surgical clips in the mediastinum. There is complete opacification of the right hemithorax due to a right pneumonectomy. The heart and mediastinum are shifted to the right. Streaky infiltrates are seen in the overexpanded left lung field. Subcutaneous emphysema is also seen over the right hemithorax.

The chest radiograph in Figure 2 (Postoperative Day 6) reveals that a 10-cm-diameter air pocket has collected in the right hemithorax raising the possibility of an air leak. There is a persistent interstitial infiltrate in the left base.

The chest radiograph in Figure 3 reveals a complete reversal of right hemithorax opacification and shift of mediastinal structures back to the midline due to development of a bronchial stump fistula.

Further Testing: Bronchoscopy was performed through the ETT in the patient's room. No obvious disruption of the right pneumonectomy stump was seen, although air bubbles were identified coming through this area. The stump area appeared yellowish and somewhat necrotic. The existing ETT was then replaced by a double-lumen ETT. After the left bronchial tree was isolated by inflation of the cuff, a fiberoptic bronchoscope (pediatric) was used to once again identify the right pneumonectomy stump. A 5-lumen pulmonary artery catheter with the distal end cut was then inserted next to the fiberoptic bronchoscope through the right bronchial tube, and 2 mL each of cryoprecipitate and thrombin were used to build up a fibrin clot over the pneumonectomy stump.

Discussion

A bronchial stump fistula (BSF) is a serious complication after pneumonectomy, and surgical repair is often difficult. A BSF occurs as a postoperative complication in some 2% of pulmonary resections.[1] Closure of the BSF can either be surgical or bronchoscopic with fibrin sealant. The latter can be accomplished at the bedside and avoids both general anesthesia and a thoracotomy.[2]

As seen in Figures 2 & 3, there is a lowering of the air-fluid level of the postpneumonectomy cavity due to fluid loss through the trachea into the contralateral bronchus. Because our patient was on positive pressure ventilation at the time of occurrence, no residual fluid was left in the pneumonectomy space. Because of intubation and sedation, our patient did not demonstrate the classic hacking cough associated with copious bloody fluid.[3]

Surgical repair of BSFs remains a viable option for postpneumonectomy patients. Long-term success rates continue to increase. Pedicle muscle-flap reinforcement has been used, which provides revascularization to promote stump healing, but success rates still average only 60% in institutions with many cases.[4,5]

High frequency ventilation (HFV) continues to be a promising therapy for the prevention of BSF.[2,6] It has also been reported to be successful for peroral sealing of bronchial stump fistulas.[2] Although the mechanisms of HFV are not clearly understood,[3] it is completely compatible with PEEP therapy, with reduced peak and main airway pressures.[6,7] Therefore, HFV may reduce the risk of barotrauma that is associated with volume ventilation. HFV has also been reported to be beneficial in the application of fibrin glue to a BSF, because the lungs hardly move during this type of ventilation, giving the physician or operator an excellent view of the working area.[2] Unfortunately, HFV equipment, despite its relatively low cost, still may not be readily available even at large institutions.[6] This is unfortunate, not only because it can be used in conjunction with bronchoscopy in applying fibrin glue to BSFs with success, but might also be used prophylactically to prevent BSFs.

REFERENCES

1. York EL, Lewall DB, Hirji M, Gelfand ET, Modry DL. Endoscopic diagnosis and treatment of postoperative bronchopleural fistula. Chest 1990;97:1390-1392.
2. Mallios C, van Stolk MA, Scheck PA, Overbeek SE, Sie TH. One lung high frequency ventilation for peroral sealing of bronchial stump fistulae. Anaesthesia 1988;43:409-410.
3. Lams P. Radiographic signs in postpneumonectomy bronchopleural fistula. J Can Assoc Radiol 1980;31:178-180.

TEST YOUR RADIOLOGIC SKILL

4. Brewer LA III. Bronchopleural fistula: management. In: Grillo HC, Eschapasse H, eds. International trends in general thoracic surgery, Vol 2. Major challenges. Philadelphia: WB Saunders, 1987:398-406.
5. Perelman MI, Rymko LP, Ambatiello GP. Bronchopleural fistual: surgery after pneumonectomy. In: Grillo HC, Eschapasse H, eds. International trends in general thoracic surgery, Vol 2. Major Challenges. Philadelphia: WB Saunders, 1987:407-412.
6. Pomerantz AH, Derasari MD, Sethi SS, Khan S. Early postpneumonectomy bronchial stump fistula. Chest 1988;93:654-657.
7. McPherson SP, Spearman CB, eds. Respiratory therapy equipment. St Louis: CV Mosby, 1990:176-178.

INSTRUCTIONS FOR AUTHORS

In addition to case reports strictly involving pulmonary medicine radiography, case reports involving pulmonary and neonatal critical-care radiography can also be submitted to the 'Test Your Radiologic Skill' corner. However, all case reports should relate somehow to respiratory care. Illustrative radiographs may be of routine chest exams or of other less-common exams such as digital subtraction or computerized axial tomography.

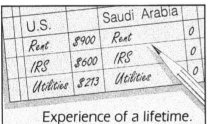

Kittredge's Corner

Richard D Branson RRT and
Robert S Campbell RRT, Section Editors

Sighs: Wasted Breath or Breath of Fresh Air?

Richard D Branson RRT and Robert S Campbell RRT

You must remember this,
A kiss is just a kiss,
A sigh is just a sigh,
The fundamental rules apply . . .

Herman Hupfeld

Background

Sigh Breath *(definition): A deliberate increase in tidal volume for one or more breaths at intervals.* During mechanical ventilation, the sigh volume generally used is twice the tidal volume.[1] Discussions in the literature concerning the sigh breath during mechanical ventilation have spawned some clever manuscript titles. These include the obvious Shakespearean takeoff "To Sigh, or Not To Sigh"[2] and the Journal's own "The Mechanical Ventilation Sigh Is a Dodo."[3] Many of you have now, doubtlessly, conjured up manuscript titles of your own (some of which may not be publishable). Mentioning a sigh probably brings to mind the ditty, reproduced above, now famous for its role in the cinema classic *Casablanca.* With that in mind, we would like to see what "fundamental rules apply" to the sigh.

As early as 1944, investigators began to report the adverse effects of prolonged immobility on pulmonary function.[4,5] Soon thereafter, several reports[6-8] demonstrated that the combination of anesthesia and immobility during prolonged operative procedures resulted in a similar deterioration in respiratory mechanics, manifested by a decrease in lung compliance, a fall in arterial oxygen content, and atelectasis. These authors agreed that the etiology was collapse of dependent lung units.

In 1959, Ferris and Pollard[9] studied the respiratory mechanics of poliomyelitis patients and found that these patients typically had a reduction in vital capacity and pulmonary compliance to

approximately 50% of normal. Ferris and Pollard suspected that immobility contributed to these derangements and theorized that periodic deep breaths might reverse a portion of the changes. With patients in tank respirators, they generated deep breaths by decreasing tank pressure by 30-35 cm H_2O and holding this pressure for 2-3 seconds. These deep breaths were provided in groups of four, with measurements of pulmonary compliance interspersed. Most patients showed a transient improvement in pulmonary compliance (10-50%) that lasted 30 minutes to 1 hour. Ferris and Pollard concluded that deep breaths "should minimize the changes in pulmonary compliance associated with severe respiratory muscular weakness due to poliomyelitis *provided it was done sufficiently often.*"[9] They also suggested that spontaneous or assisted deep breaths during postoperative recovery might reduce the incidence of atelectasis.

In that same year, Mead and Collier[10] demonstrated a progressive fall in the pulmonary compliance of anesthetized dogs allowed to breathe spontaneously or paralyzed and ventilated at a constant tidal volume. By periodically inflating the lung to a larger volume, Mead and Collier found that the fall in compliance could be completely reversed. These "sighs," or "forced inflations," were delivered every 10 minutes at a peak inflation pressure of 40 cm H_2O for 10 *seconds.* This report suggested that reductions in pulmonary compliance were the result of alveolar collapse in dependent lung units at low lung volumes that are reversed when higher lung volumes are achieved. Mead and Collier speculated that while forced inflations in anesthetized subjects had not yet been attempted, "intermittent inflation should in large part prevent compliance reductions during anesthesia."[10]

Mead and colleagues at the Massachusetts General Hospital took this concept to the operating room to test their hypothesis.[11,12] The first of these investigations studied 18 patients with normal pulmonary function requiring an operative procedure and "profound muscle relaxation" with controlled ventilation.[11] Patients were ventilated at a frequency of 20-25 breaths/min with a pressure-limited (15-20 cm H_2O) anesthesia ventilator. Tidal volume was not measured. Pulmonary compliance was measured using a super syringe, and arterial blood was analyzed. Patients initially were ventilated without periodic deep breaths; compliance and arterial blood gas values were measured every 10-30 minutes. This time served as the control period. During the second phase of the study, periodic deep breaths were delivered via manual compression of the rebreathing bag. Bendixen describes this technique: "The first inflation was carried out with a pressure of 20 cm of water, sustained for 10 seconds; the second inflation applied a pressure of 30 cm of water for 15 seconds; and the third inflation produced a pressure of 40 cm of water sustained for 15 seconds." Arterial blood gas analysis and pulmonary compliance measurements were performed before and 1 minute after each period of hyperinflation. Bendixen and colleagues[11] found a consistent fall in P_aO_2 and pulmonary compliance after 30 minutes of ventilation, which was effectively reversed by periodic hyperinflation. They concluded that when periodic deep breaths are eliminated, progressive atelectasis and intrapulmonary shunting occur. Bendixen et al suggested that periodic hyperinflations reversed these aberrations in pulmonary function and that "sighs" should become part of routine care of the anesthetized patient.

In a separate study, Bendixen et al documented the occurrence of sighs in healthy, normal volunteers.[12] This study found that an average of 9-10 sighs occurs each hour. Bendixen and colleagues, armed with the information from previous work, suggested that, aside from demonstrating emotional relief, a sigh is important in providing reinflation of atelectatic areas of the lung.[12]

Further work from the Massachusetts General Hospital in an animal model confirmed the beneficial effects of intermittent deep breaths on pulmonary compliance and P_aO_2.[13] This study also suggested that in the face of pre-existing pulmonary pathology, delivering deep breaths may not be as effective as previously demonstrated in normals.

Fletcher and Barber studied the effects of "sighing" on spontaneously breathing normals by eliminating normal sighs from the breathing pattern via an injection of morphine sulfate.[14] These authors found an increase in pulmonary compliance following a sigh, but noted that this improvement only lasted about 4 minutes. They concluded that a sigh breath changes surface-tension properties of the lung resulting in short-lived changes in compliance and that sighs do not decrease the number of unventilated alveoli.

Housley and co-workers[2] were the first to investigate use of the sigh breath in mechanically ventilated patients in the intensive care unit. Patients requiring 3-19 days on mechanical ventilation were studied, with sighs delivered at a minimum pressure of 30 cm H_2O and held "as long as possible." In most patients this time was 5-10 seconds, and the average sigh volume (2.24 L) was 2.25 times greater than set tidal volume. Housley et al failed to demonstrate any beneficial effect of sigh breaths in terms of pulmonary compliance or gas exchange. They concluded, "There seems to be no advantage in routinely administering sighs to such patients."[2]

Levine and colleagues compared the effects of sighs, large tidal volumes, and PEEP during assisted ventilation to determine their effects on blood gas values in patients with respiratory failure.[15] In concordance with Housley et al, Levine et al found no beneficial effects of sighs. This study was also one of the first to suggest that allowing the patient to determine his own respiratory frequency was beneficial and that tidal volumes of 0.7 to 1.2 L be used.

Fairley reviewed the sigh breath in 1976, panning it in the Journal.[3] Aside from questioning usefulness of the sigh, he also suggested that it may cause pulmonary barotrauma, particularly when used in patients with COPD. Fairley concluded that ventilators could be cheaper and safer without sighs. He further stated, "The sigh is dead. May it be permitted to rest in peace!"

Balsys et al,[16] using a canine model of pulmonary edema, investigated the effects of sighs on compliance, P_aO_2, and functional residual capacity (FRC). (These authors had apparently not read or decided to ignore Fairley's article of some 10 years earlier.) This report found that while compliance and FRC transiently improved following a sigh,

P_{aO_2} fell. Balsys et al concluded that when large tidal volumes are used (10-15 mL/kg) sighs are not necessary.

Ventilator Sigh-Breath Delivery

The following are descriptions of sigh-breath delivery techniques by commercially available ventilators. Table 1 lists the sigh capabilities of these ventilators.*

BEAR 1, 2, and 3

The BEAR ventilators are capable of delivering sighs in the modes called control (CMV) and assist-control (AMV). The number, volume, and frequency of sighs are adjustable on the control panel. Following delivery of a sigh breath, the ensuing expiratory time is doubled to allow for a complete exhalation. A separate high-pressure alarm is adjustable to 100 cm H_2O on the BEAR 1 and 120 cm H_2O on the BEAR 2 and 3. Sighs can be turned off, and a manual sigh can be delivered by depressing the Single Sigh button. The BEAR 1 allows a manual sigh to be delivered when the sigh function is off, while the BEAR 2 and 3 allow a manual sigh only if the sigh function is on.

BEAR 5

The BEAR 5 utilizes Sigh On and Sigh Off membrane keys to control all other sigh functions. When the Sigh Off key is depressed, sighs cannot be delivered (manual or time triggered). When the Sigh On key is depressed, sigh volume, sigh frequency, number of sighs, and sigh high-pressure alarm can be set. During CMV and AMV, following a sigh breath the normal expiratory time is doubled to allow complete expiration. In the IMV modes, the expiratory time is unaltered. In the CPAP mode (including PSV) sighs can be delivered but only one at a time.

Bird 6400ST and 8400ST

Depressing the Sigh membrane pad on the 6400ST and 8400ST activates the sigh mechanism

---

* Suppliers are identified in the Product Sources section at the end of the text.

and causes the corresponding LED (light-emitting diode) to illuminate. Sighs are always delivered singly and are available in all modes. Sigh frequency is 1 every 100 total breaths (spontaneous plus machine breaths). Sigh volume is delivered at 1.5 times the set tidal volume at the set inspiratory flowrate. This means inspiratory time increases until the sigh volume is delivered or the sigh high-pressure alarm setting is exceeded (1.5 times the normal-breath high-pressure alarm up to 140 cm H_2O). There is no maximum inspiratory time during a sigh breath. When the Sigh membrane pad is depressed, the next delivered breath is a sigh breath. No separate manual-sigh control is provided, but one can in effect deliver a manual sigh by turning the Sigh on and then off immediately following delivery of the breath.

Emerson 3MV

The Emerson 3MV does not provide for the delivery of sigh breaths.

Hamilton Veolar and Amadeus

The Hamilton ventilators can be set to deliver sighs by changing the #3 dip switch in the special-functions drawer. A sigh breath is available in all modes except PCV. A sigh breath is delivered once every 100 breaths (spontaneous and mechanical) at a tidal volume 1.5 times set tidal volume, not to exceed 2.0 L. Volume is increased by increasing inspiratory flow; inspiratory time stays constant. The high-pressure alarm during a sigh breath is raised 10 cm H_2O above the normal-breath high-pressure alarm. Manual sighs are not available.

Infrasonics Adult Star

Sighs are available in the assist/control and SIMV modes at 1-20 sighs/hour for 1, 2, or 3 breaths. Sigh volume is adjustable from 0.1 to 2.5 L but cannot exceed 1.5 times the set tidal volume. Sigh volume is increased by increasing inspiratory time while inspiratory flow remains constant. The high-pressure alarm during a sigh breath is increased to 1.5 times the normal-breath high-pressure alarm setting. Expiratory time following a sigh breath is a minimum of 0.4 seconds. During

AMV, the expiratory time is doubled to allow a complete exhalation, while in SIMV it is unchanged. Sighs can be delivered in the CPAP mode but only via a manual sigh.

Impact Uni-Vent 750

The Uni-Vent 750, a portable ventilator, delivers a sigh breath every 7 minutes or 100 breaths when the Sigh On membrane pad is activated. Sigh volume is delivered at 1.5 times set tidal volume by lengthening inspiratory time by 50% (up to a maximum of 3.0 seconds). The high-peak-pressure alarm remains the same during a sigh breath. Manual sighs are not available.

Newport E-100i

The E-100i does not deliver sighs.

Newport Breeze

The Breeze allows a sigh breath to be delivered every 100 breaths in the AMV mode only. Sigh volume is delivered at 1.5 times set tidal volume by increasing inspiratory time by 1.5. A single sigh is delivered, and inspiratory time is restricted to an I:E (ratio of inspiratory-to-expiratory time) greater than 4:1. The sigh volume range is 0.045 to 3.75 L, and the high-pressure alarm of a sigh is 1.5 times the set normal-breath high-pressure alarm.

Newport Wave

The Wave allows sighs to be delivered in the AMV or SIMV modes every 100 breaths. Sigh volume is delivered at 1.5 times set tidal volume by increasing inspiratory time by 1.5, up to an I:E of 3:1. A single sigh is delivered at a volume of 0.045-3.75 L. The high-pressure alarm does not change. A sigh can be delivered in the pressure control mode. In which case inspiratory time is increased by 150%, but the set-pressure limit remains the same.

Ohmeda Advent

The Advent utilizes a rotary control to select the sigh function, which is operable in all modes except CPAP and pressure control. A single sigh is delivered every 100 breaths at 1.5 times the set tidal volume (0.1-3.0 L) by increasing inspiratory time commensurately. Manual sighs are available. High-inspiratory-pressure alarm remains unchanged, and the maximun inspiratory time is 4.0 seconds. Following a sigh breath, expiratory time is 2 times the sigh inspiratory time.

PPG IRISA

The PPG IRISA does not provide for sighs. Instead, the IRISA utilizes an "intermittent PEEP" function set by a control knob on the faceplate of the ventilator and available only in the CMV mode. This function allows the clinician to set a second PEEP level (up to 35 cm H_2O) that increases end-expiratory pressure to that level for 2 breaths every 3 minutes. To date, evaluations of the intermittent PEEP function have not been published.

Puritan-Bennett MA-1

Sighs are adjustable on the MA-1 across a frequency range of 4-15/hour at tidal volumes of 0.1-2.2 L. A manual sigh is available, and 1-3 sighs can be delivered on each occasion. A separate high-pressure alarm is adjustable from 20-80 cm H_2O. When a sigh breath is delivered, the sigh indicator illuminates. Sigh breaths on the MA-1 are delivered at the inspiratory flowrate set on the ventilator.

Puritan-Bennett 7200ae

The 7200ae allows keyboard entry of sigh volume (0.1-2.5 L), sigh frequency (1-15/h), number of sighs (1, 2, or 3), and sigh high-pressure alarm (10-120 cm H_2O). A manual sigh is available by depressing the Manual Sigh touch pad. Volume delivery during a sigh breath is increased by lengthening inspiratory time while inspiratory flow remains constant. An indicator light illuminates when a sigh is delivered.

The 7200ae also makes automatic changes when certain ventilator settings are made: (1) If set tidal volume is increased above the sigh volume, sigh volume is automatically increased to match tidal volume. (2) If tidal volume is set to less than half the sigh volume, sigh volume is reset to 2 times the tidal volume. (3) If the normal-breath high-pressure alarm is raised above the sigh high-pressure alarm, the 7200ae readjusts the sigh high-pressure alarm to match the normal-breath high-pressure alarm.

Siemens 900C

Sighs are available only in the Volume Control + Sigh mode and are delivered at twice the set tidal volume every 100 breaths in increments of 1. A manual sigh is not available, and the high-pressure alarm remains unchanged. Volume is delivered by doubling inspiratory time. If inspiratory time exceeds 80% of cycle time, the sigh is terminated.

Siemens 300

Sighs are not available on the Siemens 300 ventilator.

Commentary

Based upon the descriptions, it is clear that a sigh is not simply a larger tidal volume. Many ventilators use elaborate schemes for sigh breaths depending upon the mode of operation, sigh settings, and related variables. Yet, based on the available literature, the sigh breath really has *no place* in the intensive care unit. Perhaps something was 'lost in the translation' when sighs were integrated into mechanical ventilators. We have seen that in the operating room where sighs are delivered and held for 10-15 seconds. And while this may re-expand atelectatic areas in dependent lung regions, this is not what mechanical ventilators do! Simply increasing the tidal volume by 1.5 or 2 times and extending inspiratory time cannot mimic what our anesthesia colleagues have described.

Furthermore, while we can conclude that the sigh is unnecessary when large tidal volumes (9-12 mL/kg) are delivered, we may also speculate that sighs may be dangerous. Our understanding of the physiologic derangements in the adult respiratory distress syndrome (ARDS) and respiratory failure in patients with COPD has increased markedly since the last of the studies on sighs was published (1980). We have come to understand that while portions of the lung are severely affected, other areas remain relatively normal. This heterogenous distribution results in maldistribution of delivered tidal volume to the non-dependent, more normal regions of the lung, predisposing the patient to pulmonary barotrauma. If we deliver sighs in this situation, at 15-20 mL/kg, we may compound the risk of barotrauma.

We have also wondered how patient-ventilator synchrony is affected by an arbitrary doubling of inspiratory time. To date, this has not been studied or reported.

Of course, there may yet be a place for the sigh breath. It can be argued that, during IMV at low respiratory frequency, the mandatory breaths are sighs interspersed with the patient's spontaneous breathing. We have recently begun using sighs during pressure support ventilation (PSV). In weaning patients with PSV, we have observed that as tidal volume approaches the 4-6 mL/kg range, mild hypoxemia occurs in some instances. We have anecdotal evidence of our ability to reverse these falling P_aO_2s by adding sigh breaths at 12 mL/kg, 6-10 times/hour. It is unclear whether we could have effected the same changes by increasing the PSV level or PEEP. We feel the use of sighs during PSV warrants further study.

Despite possibly appropriate future uses, at this time we believe the sigh breath should be avoided in critically ill, mechanically ventilated patients. Not only has its efficacy not been proven, but strong evidence suggests that it is uncomfortable at best and potentially dangerous. Three of the 20 ventilators we have described do not have a sigh option. We are unsure if the addition of the sigh option is expensive; but, we believe that with the complexity of today's ventilators, an option without usefulness should not take up space on the control panel. Of course, some clinicians, with questionable habits of the past engrained, will continue to insist that manufacturers provide this option. We implore you to read the references for yourself and come to a logical conclusion based on the facts.

PRODUCT SOURCES

BEAR 1, 2, 3, and 5, Bear Medical Systems Inc, Riverside CA
Bird 6400ST and 8400ST, Bird Products Corp, Palm Springs CA
Emerson 3MV, JH Emerson Co, Cambridge MA
Hamilton Veolar and Amadeus, Hamilton Medical, Reno NV
Infrasonics Adult Star, Infrasonics Inc, San Diego CA
Impact Uni-Vent 750, Impact Medical, West Caldwell NJ
Newport E-100i, Breeze, and Wave, Newport Medical Instruments Inc, Newport Beach CA
Ohmeda Advent, Ohmeda, Columbia MD
PPG IRISA, PPG Biomedical Systems, Lenexa KS
Puritan-Bennett MA-1 and 7200ae, Puritan-Bennett, Carlsbad CA
Siemens 900C and 300, Siemens Life Support Systems, Iselin NJ

REFERENCES

1. Chatburn RL, Lough MD, Primiano FP Jr. Mechanical ventilation. In: Chatburn RL, Lough MD, eds. Handbook of respiratory care. Chicago: Year Book Medical Publishers Inc, 1990:159-224.
2. Housley E, Louzda N, Becklake MR. To sigh or not to sigh. Am Rev Respir Dis 1970;101:611-614.
3. Fairley HB. The mechanical ventilation sigh is a dodo. Respir Care 1976;21:1127-1130.
4. Dock W. The evil sequelae of complete bed rest. JAMA 1944;125:1083-1088.
5. Harrison TR. Abuse of rest as a therapeutic measure for patients with cardiovascular disease. JAMA 1944;125:1075-1082.
6. Drinker CK, Hardenbergh E. The effects of the supine position upon the ventilation of the lungs of dogs. Surgery 1948;24:113-118.
7. Colville P, Shugg C, Ferris BG. Effects of body tilting on respiratory mechanics. J Appl Physiol 1956;9;19-24.
8. Howell JBL, Peckett BW. Studies of the elastic properties of the thorax of supine anaesthetized paralysed human subjects. J Physiol 1957;136:1-19.
9. Ferris BG, Pollard DS. Effect of deep and quiet breathing on pulmonary compliance in man. J Clin Invest 1960;39:143-149.
10. Mead J, Collier C. Relation of volume history of lungs to respiratory mechanics in anesthetized dogs. J Appl Physiol 1959;14:669-678.
11. Bendixen HH, Hedley-Whyte J, Lauer MB. Impaired oxygenation in surgical patients during general anesthesia with controlled ventilation. N Engl J Med 1963;269:991-996.
12. Bendixen HH, Smith G, Mead J. Pattern of ventilation in young adults. J Appl Physiol 1963;19:195-198.
13. Lauer MB, Morgan J, Bendixen HH, Radford EP. Lung volume, compliance and arterial oxygen tensions during controlled ventilation. J Appl Physiol 1964;19:725-733.
14. Fletcher G, Barber JL. Lung mechanics and physiologic shunt during spontaneous breathing in normal subjects. Anesthesiology 1966;27:638-647.
15. Levine M, Gilbert R, Auchincloss JH. A comparison of the effects of sighs, large tidal volumes and positive end expiratory pressure in assisted ventilation. Scand J Respir Dis 1972;53:101-108.
16. Balsys AJ, Jones RL, Man SFP, Wells A. Effects of sighs and different tidal volumes on compliance, functional residual capacity and arterial oxygen tension in normal and hypoxemic dogs. Crit Care Med 1980;8:641-645.

Send submissions to RESPIRATORY CARE, Technical Corner Editors, 11030 Ables Lane, Dallas TX 75229.

For direct consultation with Section Editors, send fax to Richard D Branson & Robert S Campbell, (513) 558-3474.

Reprints: Richard D Branson RRT, Dept of Surgery, Univ of Cincinnati Medical Ctr, 231 Bethesda Ave, Cincinnati OH 45267-0558.

The best monitor is a reliable monitor. MiniOX® oxygen monitors deliver month after month of accurate readings with virtually no instrument downtime.

At the heart of MiniOX reliability is the most durable oxygen sensor made. It's warrantied for a full year. While other oxygen monitor manufacturers may offer similar warranties, the actual MiniOX performance record is outstanding.

MiniOX oxygen sensors exceed their warrantied lifetime. That means no instrument downtime! And that also makes MSA Catalyst Research the *only* choice when you do need to change sensors for the MiniOX you already own.

MiniOX electronics are superior, too. Designed simply, yet built for demanding applications, they are trouble-free. Powered by a standard 9V alkaline battery, they are also convenient to maintain.

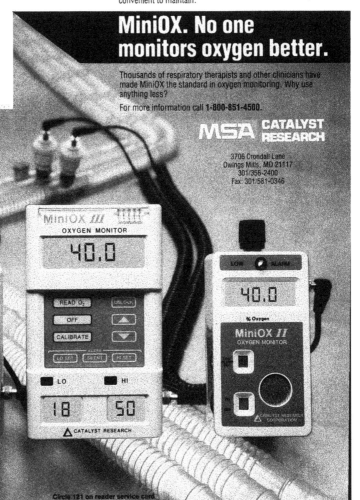
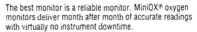

Books, Films Tapes, & Software

Listing and Reviews of Books and Other Media
Note to publishers: Send review copies of books, films, tapes, and software to
RESPIRATORY CARE, 11030 Ables Lane, Dallas TX 75229-4593

"Pickwickian" and Other Stories of Intensive Care, by Lawrence Martin MD. Softcover, 246 pages. Lakeside Press, 5124 Mayfield Rd, #191, Cleveland OH 44124. 1-800-247-6553. $10.95.

As an editor aware that some book titles beckon the reader, while others mystify him, I like Dr Martin's title for his book. If you are a medical worker who knows what "Pickwickian" means, you will want to open this book because these patients are always fascinating. Even if you have encountered one or more of them in the past, you will be very much interested in another. If you are a layperson, the title will pull you in, too—because you have some idea what intensive care is, and you wonder what the heck "Pickwickian" is.

Attracted by the book's good title, you turn to the Table of Contents and are lured by chapters called Rounds, Overdose, Medicine by Default, Strange Pneumonia, Asthma in the Last Trimester, "We can't kill your mother!," The Yellow Man, Adult Respiratory Distress, Too Much Sugar—Too Little History, Crusade, "Just give me a cigarette," Pickwickian, Coma, Cocaine Wins, Crisis and Lysis, Extraordinary Care, Thyroid Storm, From ARC to AIDS, As High as a Giraffe's, and Ascending Weakness. I cite the entire contents in order to show that there is something for everybody. Unlike the book's title, some of these chapter headings are not always clues to their topics—but this provides us the fun of trying to guess. What, for example, can Medicine by Default mean? Or As High as a Giraffe's? We have to find out—and so we buy the book.

What sort of readers did the author have in mind when he put this book together? The preface begins

with the question, "Did you ever wonder what happens when a patient enters 'Intensive Care'? What goes on behind those doors marked *AUTHORIZED PERSONNEL ONLY?"* Clearly, then, the book is intended for the lay reader. This is emphasized later in the preface, where the author states that "Medical jargon is kept to a necessary minimum and most unfamiliar terms are described or defined when introduced; a Glossary is also provided at the end of the book."

Nevertheless, I found that even though my medical affiliation means I am not a lay reader, I thoroughly enjoyed this work. Dr Martin did not 'write down' to the lay reader; in fact, I suspect that to a certain extent he forgot that reader and just let his stories come out, with happy results.

What, then, is it like for a medical worker to read this book? I was fascinated. When I read about a patient with Guillain-Barré syndrome, my mind flew back almost 30 years, and I saw again, very clearly, the first G-B patient I encountered, a healthy looking man in his late 20s. Even his name had stayed in my head—and I remembered how I shared the fear that he and his family felt. So, one effect of Dr Martin's stories is to stir up old, rich memories in a person who is familiar with the ICU world.

I learned stuff, too. Concerning asthma, Dr Martin tells us, "To gain some idea of what it feels like during an asthma attack, try breathing through a straw with your nose plugged." Nothing new so far; I used to have my students do that. But then he goes farther: "As you breathe, gradually pinch the middle of the straw until it closes about half way. Now jog in place." That part is new to me; jogging wasn't 'in' when I was teaching. So just now I tried the jogging-cum-straw experiment. Hey!

that's really uncomfortable. Something else I didn't know: Dr Martin has noticed that many elderly patients in the ICU tend not to ask questions about their disease or prognosis; they seem not to want to know. I never would have guessed that.

History rears its interesting head here and there. We learn that the intracardiac catheter technique was invented in 1929, then lay dormant until the 1940s. And before insulin therapy became available, the treatment for diabetes was *starvation.*

What reading this book would be like for a lay reader, I can only guess. One attractive feature is that the book really is a series of mystery stories. The common technique in these tales is this: (1) Dr Martin introduces the patient, giving us a few clues to his or her appearance, history, and current complaint; (2) then he leaves the patient for a bit in order to explain some relevant medical technology; and (3) he comes back to the patient and relates how the technology solves the mystery and/or tries to help the patient. It's an effective writing approach; I was never bored for a moment.

Dr Martin's use of language pleased me. After a patient had received five different antibiotics, the author remarks that "Any common or typical infection should have been clobbered." This doctor is no stuffed shirt and like his colleagues, you could comfortably call him Larry. I particularly enjoyed a line that might have come from TV sports commentator John Madden: "End-stage alcoholics with esophageal bleeding all wear football helmets in the ICU!"

Larry's regular-guy frailty shows too. He recounts how during rounds on a comatose patient a nurse found it necessary to interrupt him and ask whether they shouldn't leave the room before talking about that patient.

The writing/reading pace is fine. The sentences are not too long. Not so short as Hemingway's, but just right. They segue into one another smoothly and naturally. I think the secret is that the good doctor writes as though he were talking to the staff during ICU rounds.

Effective figures of speech abound. Here's one: "Today, caring for critically ill patients without blood gas measurements would seem like driving fast in a dense fog. You might make it, but you would probably crash."

Not all words that might faze the lay reader made it into the glossary. "Teratogenic effects" is an example. Somewhere else I noticed the medical use of "insult," which might make the lay reader raise his eyebrows. It's not in the glossary, either. Nor is "apnea" explained. But not all such terms could be explained— there are too many. Luckily, the stories are so interesting that I doubt a lay reader would worry about an unfamiliar word now and then.

All of us who have worked in hospitals have stories to tell, and some of them may surface as we read Dr Martin's tales. I recalled a 107-year-old COPDer who liked to give advice. "When you go bear-hunting," he told me one day, "always keep your dog downhill from the bear. If'n he's uphill, the bear'll get him sure." (I promised I would remember.) Dr Martin's stories are true, they are well told, and some of them also contain what can be taken as advice. After reading The Yellow Man, you may never take another drink. Bear-hunting is safer.

A generous author, who doesn't seek to keep his readers for himself only, Dr Martin concludes his book with a bibliography of 11 books and articles that are first-person accounts

by others—physicians and nurses. One—The Three Legged Stallion and Other Tales from a Doctor's Notebook—sounds too good to be missed. Thanks, Larry.

I don't know how common this experience is, but when I am nearing the end of a really good book, I may become irritated with the author— even mad at him—because the book will soon end, whereas I'd like it to go on forever. I got mad at Dr Martin about halfway through "As High as a Giraffe's"—because I was past Page 200, and not much lay ahead.

Do I recommend this book? Absolutely—not only to the intelligent and curious lay reader, but certainly to respiratory care practitioners, and particularly to students. If I were an educator, I would assign its various chapters for student reading at appropriate stages in the curriculum. If I were a clinical department head, "Pickwickian" would be in the departmental library.

Philip Kittredge RRT
Adjunct Editor
RESPIRATORY CARE
Little River, California

ECG Essentials: A Pocket Reference for Systematic Interpretation, by Kent R Murphy MD and Jeffrey J Pelton MD. Spiralbound, soft-cover, illustrated, 176 pages. Chicago: Quintessence Publishing Co Inc, 1991. $24.00.

Numerous technologic advances in clinical electrocardiography have occurred in recent years, providing the clinician with a systematic method of ECG interpretation that allows for the effective management and treatment of potentially life-threatening arrhythmias. While the method of interpretation of the standard 12-lead electrocardiogram has remained generally unchanged, the use of the electrocardiogram as a

diagnostic tool has lead to an improved understanding of both basic and complex electrophysiology. The primary aim of this text, as noted by its authors, is to present a "simple, reproducible and rapidly applicable method for ECG interpretation, which will prepare the student for more advanced, future studies in electrophysiology."

This pocket manual is divided into 8 chapters: "Basic Principles of Cardiac Electrophysiology," "Evaluating Rate," "Evaluating Rhythm," "Intervals and Waveforms," "Rhythm, Interval, and Waveform Pathology," "Evaluating Axis," "Evaluating Cardiac Anatomy," "Screening for Ischemia and Infarction," and "Special Topics: Pericarditis, Pulmonary Embolism, and Pacemakers." This organization of topics leads the student in a systematic manner from understanding the hexaxial reference system introduced by Robert Grant in the 1950s through the identification of pathology that can be identified with the aid of the electrocardiogram. Each chapter contains sufficient information to provide a fundamental understanding of electrocardiography; additionally, each chapter is supplemented with ECG tracings and review questions to enhance the educational process. Appendices include answers to review questions, ACLS protocols, descriptions of performing central venous access and pericardiocentesis, guidelines for the administration of antiarrhythmic drugs, and normal hemodynamic and laboratory values.

Although this manual is relatively free of grammatical errors, errors in typesetting and mislabeling of tracings and diagrams are apparent (Page 13, the numerical order of the outline is incorrect; Page 87, the subject heading 'Pacemaker' is omitted; Page 166 contains a typographical error; in Figure 1-3 labeling of the diagram is not complete; Figure 4-21 contains a typographical error; and in Figure 4-28, ECG is mislabeled). In addition,

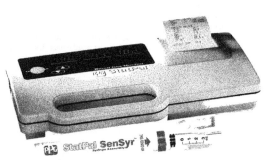

several content areas would have benefitted from the presentation of additional information or perhaps the selection of clearer, more descriptive ECG samples to complement the text. The authors' description of supraventricular tachycardia (SVT) clearly states that this is a rapid heart rate of 150-250 beats/minute. The ECG example (Fig. 4-24) used to illustrate SVT is 100 beats/minute. I believe that the discussion of heart block should include additional examples of second-degree heart block to demonstrate fixed conduction patterns such as 2:1 or 3:1. These additions might enhance the student's understanding of impulse conduction and also aid in understanding the terminology used to describe the various forms of heart block. Within the "Special Topics" chapter, I believe that the content on pacemakers should be expanded into a complete chapter. This would provide the reader with the ability to recognize and understand the mechanisms of pacemaker failure, atrial pacing, and ventricular pacing on the electrocardiogram. To the appendices, I suggest adding a glossary of terms, diagrams to supplement central venous catheter and pericardiocentesis procedures, and equations to measure gas exchange and oxygen transport.

A problem with this text and seemingly inherent among ECG textbooks is the reproduction quality of ECG tracings (Fig. 4-7). In many instances, this problem is not the fault of the author(s), but represents the inability of the publishing company to scan and reproduce images in halftones. As a result, ECG tracings are often difficult to visualize and interpret. While actual patient electrocardiograms are generally preferred, detailed ECG tracings obtained from an ECG simulator are possible and would provide the student the opportunity to view the "perfect" example of any electrocardiogram abnormality.

Overall, this reference manual is a concise well-written guide to understanding the basics of electrocardiography. The material presented is easy to comprehend and would be beneficial to those allied health students who are interested in ECG analysis and interpretation. It is important to mention that this book was designed to provide only the "essentials" of ECG analysis; it was not the intent of the authors to provide an in-depth study of this topic. As a result, topics such as Einthoven's equation, Kirchoff's laws, and intracellular action potentials (all of which I consider of extreme importance in developing a strong foundation in the understanding and interpretation of electrocardiograms) are omitted. Finally, as in any circumstance, the reader (purchaser) should consider the cost, educational value of the product, and his/her personal interest prior to purchasing.

John M Palmisano RRT
Clinical Research Associate
Pediatric Intensive Care
CS Mott Children's Hospital
Ann Arbor, Michigan

Chairobics Video Exercise Program, created and produced by Cheryl Spessert RN. Video, 115 minutes. Sponsored by Glasrock Home Health Care. $32.95 (includes shipping and handling). Chairobics, 1410 Woodland Dr, St Louis MO 63117. 1-800-521-7303.

The **Chairobics Video Exercise Program** is an innovative adjunct to pulmonary rehabilitation. The video includes a 40-minute exercise component, 55-minute instructional section, and two 10-minute relaxation segments. Cheryl Spessert, a pulmonary nurse-clinician at Washington University School of Medicine, is its creator and executive producer. The exercise session is led by Kat Wil-

liams, an instructor certified through the American Council on Exercise. Five pulmonary patients (three men and two women) are shown exercising, one wearing a nasal cannula.

In the video, Ms Spessert encourages participants to seek physician approval and obtain an oxygen prescription for exercise, if appropriate, before beginning the program. She also encourages first-time users to view the instructional section first, to pace themselves, and to listen to their bodies. An explanation of the Borg Perceived Level of Exertion Scale follows. It is suggested that participants should expect to become "a little winded," but remain able to carry on a conversation, and that they might find it helpful to use a bronchodilator MDI prior to exercise. Heart rates are taken routinely for 10 seconds, the recommended interval due to frequent miscalculations with 6-second counts, whereas a rapidly declining heart rate is taken for 15 seconds. Spessert demonstrates how and where to take a pulse and explains how to calculate maximal heart rate (MHR) and target heart rate (using 70-80% of MHR). The explanation is easy to follow, and a video pause is suggested to give the participant time to practice bis/her own calculations. Spessert also cautions that resting heart rates for those individuals taking certain cardiac medications may be as much as 20 beats/minute higher, and recommends that participants who may be affected by this receive specific advice from their physician. Participants are advised to stop exercising if they experience dizziness, fatigue, excessive shortness of breath, or chest pain. Spessert encourages participants to start slowly and not to expect to complete the entire session the first time, but rather to increase the session length as their strength and endurance increase.

The video contains all of the standard components for a complete workout—stretching, strength training, cardiovascular conditioning, and cooling down. Insets in the corner of the screen during the exercise session remind exercisers about such things as pursed-lip breathing, proper posture, and not stretching to the point of pain, and also instruct viewers in how to increase or decrease intensity. (Heart rates are monitored throughout the program.) Participants use 16-ounce soda bottles for hand-held weights, beginning with empty containers that are filled with water and then sand, to increase their weight as participants progress. Participants exercise to Broadway show tunes, and seem to genuinely enjoy the music—they are observed on many occasions tapping their feet as they exercise. At the segment's end, participants are reminded that their heart rate and perceived level of exertion should return to pre-exercise status; they are advised to complete one of the segments on relaxation if their pulse has not returned to its resting rate.

Two relaxation segments are offered—one portrays visual images such as the ocean and sunrise, and breathing-exercise instructions are given by a soothing voice that can be heard over the sound of sea gulls and waves breaking. The second takes the participant through progressive relaxation, alternately tensing and relaxing the major muscle groups from head to toe.

The 55-minute education component covers topics such as the disease process involved in COPD (which includes anatomic illustrations), medications, and methods of administration, including visual displays and demonstrations; a demonstration of breathing retraining; postural drainage and percussion, showing four basic positions; and smoking cessation, which directs the smoker to obtain additional information from one of several sources (American Lung Association, American Heart Association, American Cancer Society). This instruction is

followed by useful tips on energy conservation, from using paper plates during periods of fatigue, to proper body mechanics, to use of a chair in the shower. Spessert further stresses the importance of exercise at any level to increase functional capabilities. The instructional component also offers suggestions to help avoid infection (ie, influenza vaccination, proper nutrition, and hydration), and describes the various types of oxygen systems as they are shown on the screen. Spessert concludes the instructional segment by advising participants that duration of exercise is more important than intensity and that they should increase duration first, followed by intensity, once they are able to complete the entire program. Exercisers are encouraged to participate in some type of aerobic activity three times per week at a minimum, with four to six times being ideal. The tape is designed to be used in conjunction with walking, stationary cycling, swimming, or other forms of low-impact aerobic activity.

Chairobics is original and educational; it's about time pulmonary rehabilitation was included in the video approach to fitness. I believe that the program is an excellent adjunct to pulmonary rehabilitation for patients who have completed a structured program and who want to continue receiving its benefits.

Crystal L Dunlevy EdD RRT
Assistant Professor
Respiratory Therapy Division
School of Allied Medical Professions
Columbus, Ohio

Pulmonary Therapy and Rehabilitation: Principles and Practice, 2nd ed, edited by Francois Haas PhD and Kenneth Axen PhD. Hardcover, illustrated, 395 pages. Baltimore: Williams & Wilkins, 1991. $65.00.

The stated purpose of the editors of **Pulmonary Therapy and Reha-**

bilitation: Principles and Practice is to maximize assistance to pulmonary patients by producing "as comprehensive a book as possible." To that end, they have taken a team approach to pulmonary therapy and rehabilitation and have incorporated chapters by contributors from a variety of disciplines.

The book is divided into two sections containing 21 chapters, and contains a concise Table of Contents. All chapters provide excellent referencing and footnotes where applicable, and pertinent illustrations and tables are used throughout the book.

The first section of the book (Principles) deals with the principles of pulmonary therapy and rehabilitation. In the preface, the editors note that they want to "ground this book in physiology" in order to provide practitioners with a foundation for more effective use of rehabilitation techniques. Chapters 1 and 2 review respiratory and exercise physiology; however, these chapters are filled with formulas, symbols, and tables, and are so crammed with detail that reading is difficult and continuity is lost. Additionally, Chapter 2 contains historical excerpts that do not enhance the reader's understanding of the material and further break the flow of information. For instance, the following quote on Page 68 preceded information provided on skeletal muscle. "By the help of our more perfect glass, there met the eye vessels joining together in ring-like fashion. And such is the wandering about of these vessels, as they proceed on this side from the artery, that the vessels no longer maintain a straight direction, but there appears a network made up of the articulations of the two vessels. Hence it was clear to the senses that the blood flowed away along tortuous vessels and was not poured into spaces but was always contained within tubules. (Marcello Malpighi, 1628-1694)" The authors then proceed to discuss oxygenation and its relevance to skeletal muscle.

Other chapters in the Principles section, for the most part, are easy to read. Chapter 6 synthesizes exercise stress testing, provides helpful protocol tables and interpretations for test results, and suggests possible reasons for abnormal values. An excellent anecdote written by an ex-smoker for Chapter 7, Smoking Cessation, succinctly sums up the various means and methods available for trying to stop smoking.

Section II of the book looks at the practical aspects of pulmonary therapy and rehabilitation, starting with a chapter on the history of pulmonary rehabilitation. In addition to COPD, there are chapters on pulmonary rehabilitation for pediatric patients with asthma and cystic fibrosis and paralytic and restrictive pulmonary syndromes. A common thread of understanding is woven through this section. Contributors focus on the

---

LAST CALL FOR 1992 OPEN FORUM

It's time to submit your abstracts for possible presentation at the OPEN FORUM during the AARC Annual Meeting in San Antonio, Texas, December 12-15,

Deadline for submission is June 6. See Page 484 of this issue for more information.

---

goal of returning the patient to his/ her highest possible functional capacity through individualization of programs and regimens, and reiterate that everyone responds differently depending on circumstances. Salient points (such as disease characterization) are reinforced throughout the chapters. In Chapter 11 there is relevant discussion of why, possibly, there is skepticism about pulmonary rehabilitation programs. Where material overlaps, there is good referral to other chapters, rather than repetition of the facts.

The intended audience for **Pulmonary Therapy and Rehabilitation: Principles and Practice** is the pulmonary rehabilitation team, which includes "physician, physical therapist, respiratory therapist, vocational counselor, psychological counselor, and social worker." The editors and contributors present considerable information related to pulmonary therapy and rehabilitation that should be helpful to clinicians.

Chris Kelly BA RCP RRT
Oakland, California

The Strategic Health Care Manager: Mastering Essential Leadership Skills, by George H Stevens. Hardcover, illustrated, 277 pages. San Francisco: Jossey-Bass Inc, 1991. $33.95.

The Strategic Health Care Manager is written for the experienced clinician who has been thrust into a middle-management position for the first time and has no formal management education or management experience. Minimal technical language makes the text easy to read. Because of the author's writing style, this is one of few management books that I have read with genuine interest. The author builds a strong rapport with the reader by focusing on all appropriate topics in management, but writing on the novice's

level, and using numerous examples to illustrate key concepts.

The first chapter sets the perspective for the reader by highlighting the most recent and significant changes in the health care industry, and then the author describes how these changes have impacted the middle manager. The remaining chapters concentrate on essential aspects of sound management (namely, leadership, communication, strategic planning, project management, team building, training, performance, and, finally, development into high-level management). Any clinician-turned-supervisor will benefit from reading this book, which I hesitate to call a text because of its free-flowing style. There are a minimal number of graphs and charts to study, an average of two per chapter; they are, however, useful and illustrative.

The author skillfully whets interest in further reading and often cites references found in a special section at the end of the book (approximately 60 are listed). Four "resources" are appended to the end of the book: (1) an outline of competency areas for health care managers, (2) a competency worksheet, (3) an individual development plan, and (4) a case study.

One final note of interest is that George H Stevens, the author, is a former respiratory therapist and associate director for education for the American College of Healthcare Executives. He is currently a partner in Integrated Performance Designs, which provides services for performance systems design, performance improvement (computer-based), management and technical skill systems design, and competency-based employee development.

Keith R Momii MA MMSc
RPFT RRT
Education Coordinator
Pulmonary Care Services
University of Texas
Medical Branch
Galveston, Texas

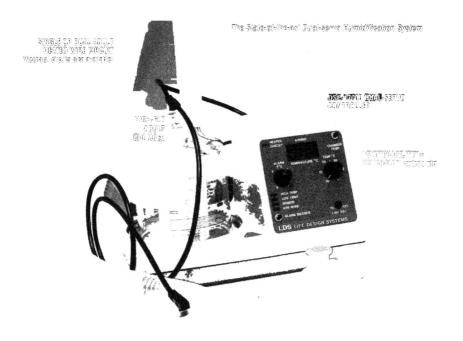

Letter on topics of current interest or commenting on material in RESPIRATORY CARE, will be considered for publication The Editors may accept or decline a letter or edit without changing the author's views. The content of letters as published may simply reflect the author's opinion or inter-pretation of information—not standard practice or the Journal's recommendation. Authors of critized material will have the opportunity to reply in print. No anonymous letters can be published. Type letter double spaced, mark it "For Publication," and mail it to RESPIRATORY CARE Journal, 11030 Ables Lane. Dallas, TX 75229-4593.

Letters

Calculating F_{DO_2} for Mixtures of Air and Oxygen

The need to combine air and oxygen frequently arises during anesthesia and critical care. Primarily, the nitrogenous component of air functions to reduce the concentration of oxygen and to decrease the risk of oxygen toxicity.[1] This dilution is also mandatory during laser surgery because high concentrations of oxygen support combustion.[2-4] Use of 100% oxygen also can result in absorption atelectasis.[5] The oxygen concentration delivered (F_{DO_2}), when air and oxygen are mixed, is calculated by Equation 1

$$F_{DO_2} = \frac{(1.0)(\dot{V}_{O_2}) + (0.21)(\dot{V}_{air})}{\dot{V}_{O_2} + \dot{V}_{air}}.$$

where $\dot{V}_{O_2} = O_2$ flowrate and

$\dot{V}_{air} = air$ flowrate.

If the flowrates of air and O_2 are known, the F_{DO_2} can be quickly calculated by Equation 2

$$F_{DO_2} = (0.79)\left(\frac{\dot{V}_{O_2}}{\dot{V}_{total}}\right) + 0.21.$$

where $\dot{V}_{total}$ = the total flowrate ($\dot{V}_{air} + \dot{V}_{O_2}$).

As shown in the Appendix, Equation 2 is just a simplified form of Equation 1. It is especially practical for rapid estimates and often can be used without a calculator. All flowrates must be in the same units (ordinarily mL · min⁻¹ or L · min⁻¹). F_{DO_2} is the fraction of the total gas flow that is oxygen. The coefficients of the equation, 0.79 and 0.21, correspond to the percentage of nitrogen and oxygen in air, respectively. Equation 2 can be easily rearranged

to solve for $\dot{V}_{O_2}$. Example: With an air flowrate of 4.5 L · min⁻¹ and oxygen flow of 0.5 L · min⁻¹ (total flow, or $\dot{V}_{total}$ = 5 L · min⁻¹, the resulting F_{DO_2} is

$$0.79\left(\frac{0.5}{5}\right) + 0.21 = 0.29,$$

ie, the oxygen fraction.

An estimate can be obtained by rounding off 0.79 to 0.80 and 0.21 to 0.20 and, in this example 0.5/5 = 0.1 and thus

$$(0.80)(0.1) + 0.20 = 0.28,$$

ie, the oxygen fraction.

By making use of simple arithmetic shortcuts, the reader can make this method work expeditiously. By Equation 1, it may be difficult to determine $\dot{V}_{O_2}$ for a given F_{DO_2}, but Equation 2 can be easily manipulated to solve for $\dot{V}_{O_2}$.

$$\dot{V}_{O_2} = \frac{(\dot{V}_{total})(F_{DO_2} - 0.21)}{0.79}.$$

Example: For an F_{DO_2} of 0.3 (30% O_2), with $\dot{V}_{total}$ of 8 L · min⁻¹, the flowrate for O_2 will be

$$\frac{(8)(0.3 - 0.21)}{0.79} = 0.91 \text{ L} \cdot \text{min}^{-1}.$$

Again, rounding off and knowing that 8/0.8 = 10 and 0.3 - 0.21 = 0.09, the solution can be estimated

$$\left(\frac{8}{0.8}\right)(0.3 - 0.21) = 0.9 \text{ L} \cdot \text{min}^{-1}$$

$\dot{V}_{air}$ can be determined by subtracting the flowrate of O_2 from the $\dot{V}_{total}$ ($\dot{V}_{air}$ = $\dot{V}_{total} - \dot{V}_{O_2}$). In the preceding example, the flowrate for air would be 8.0 – 0.91 = 7.09 L · min⁻¹. Use of these equations should reduce the 'trial and error' (and anxiety!) associated with setting air and oxygen flowrates.

Glen Atlas MD MSc
Resident
Department of Anesthesiology
SUNY Health Science Center
Syracuse, New York

REFERENCES

1. Klein J. Normobaric pulmonary oxygen toxicity. Anesth Analg 1990;70:195-207.
2. Macintosh R, Mushin WW, Epstein HG. Deflagrations and detonations in fuel mixtures. Physics for the anaesthetist. 3rd edition. Oxford: Blackwell Scientific Publications, 1963:326-357.
3. Wolf GL, Simpson JI. Flammability of endotracheal tubes in oxygen and nitrous oxide enriched atmospheres. Anesthesiology 1987;67: 236-239.
4. Schramm VL Jr, Mattox DE, Stool SE. Acute management of laser-ignited intratracheal explosion. Laryngoscope 1989;91(9, Part 1): 1417-1426.
5. Nunn JF. Applied respiratory physiology, 3rd edition. London: Butterworth & Co, 1987:442-443.

APPENDIX

Equation 2 can be derived from Equation 1 by simple algebra. First, $\dot{V}_{O_2}$ can be expressed as the sum of two fractions (0.79)($\dot{V}_{O_2}$) and (0.21) ($\dot{V}_{O_2}$).

$$F_{DO_2} = \frac{1.0)(\dot{V}_{O_2}) + (0.21)(\dot{V}_{air})}{\dot{V}_{O_2} + \dot{V}_{air}} =$$

$$\frac{(0.79 + 0.21)(\dot{V}_{O_2}) + (0.21)(\dot{V}_{air})}{\dot{V}_{O_2} + \dot{V}_{air}}.$$

Because both $\dot{V}_{O_2}$ and $\dot{V}_{air}$ are multiplied by a factor of 0.21, they can be collected. The term [$\dot{V}_{O_2}$ + $\dot{V}_{air}$] then is eliminated from both numerator and denominator of that part of the equation:

$$F_{DO_2} = \frac{(0.79)(\dot{V}_{O_2})}{\dot{V}_{O_2} + \dot{V}_{air}} + \frac{(0.21)(\dot{V}_{O_2} + \dot{V}_{air})}{\dot{V}_{O_2} + \dot{V}_{air}}$$

$$= \frac{(0.79)(\dot{V}_{O_2})}{\dot{V}_{O_2} + \dot{V}_{air}} + 0.21$$

Replacing [$\dot{V}_{O_2} + \dot{V}_{air}$] with the equation $\dot{V}_{total} = \dot{V}_{O_2} + \dot{V}_{air}$ yields the simplified result:

$$F_{DO_2} = (0.79)\left(\frac{\dot{V}_{O_2}}{\dot{V}_{total}}\right) + 0.21.$$

Professional Literacy Revisited

Last Fall Semester (1991), my students and I read with interest Robert Weilacher's editorial in RESPIRATORY CARE entitled "Professional Literacy."[1] I feel it professionally incumbent upon me to add some comments.

I have taught two advanced-level Respiratory Therapist reading courses (REST 2525 and REST 2526) in our Registry Curriculum every year for the past 19 years. In those courses, my students and I have read and evaluated practically every article published in RESPIRATORY CARE since 1972. I want to reassure my fellow Texan from Palestine that at least one academic educator not only uses but relies on RESPIRATORY CARE in his work!

I (and my students) have never seen the quality of articles in the Journal as good as they are at present. We are proud to be a part of a profession from whose peers such high quality, original, and scholarly work as that published in RESPIRATORY CARE this past year can be generated. The recent academic quality reflected in our monthly science journal should make each member of the Journal's Editorial Board proud —especially because it makes AARC members and respiratory care students proud.

I totally agree with Mr Weilacher that the Journal is *the* one tool always available to me and my stu-dents in that "constant struggle to remain professionally contem-porary."[1] Permit me to illustrate: This Spring Semester (1992), one of the topics emphasized in my course is mechanical ventilation. What a quality synthesis of up-to-date infor-mation awaited us in the Journal papers by such internationally acclaimed authors as Richard Bran-son RRT, Robert Chatburn RRT, Roger Goldberg MD, Dean Hess MEd RRT, Robert Kacmarek PhD RRT, and David Pierson MD—just to name a few! In Volume 36 (1991), topics related to mechanical ventila-tion ranged from ventilator per-formance during hyperbaric com-pression to bronchodilator admin-istration, circuit compression vol-ume, and patient work of breathing, and numbered more than 35—not including letters! My students and I found the Chatburn paper[2] on ven-tilator classification to be the single, most helpful paper published in the past 10 years.

I think that sometimes we take our Journal too much for granted; too often we do not take the time to pat on the back those who continuously produce a high quality product year after year. I have certainly failed to do so in times past, and my students and I simply want to express our thanks to the Editorial Board and the Journal's authors for adding so much to our professional enrichment and pride.

Ralph E Bartel MEd RCP RRT
Department Head
Respiratory Therapist (REST)
Program
Houston Community College

1. Weilacher R. Professional literacy (editorial). Respir Care 1991;36: 1083-1084.
2. Chatburn R L. A new system for understanding mechanical ventila-tors. Respir Care 1991;36:872-874.

Up to your neck in CLIA issues?

Ciba Corning has <u>solutions</u>.

Quality control products and data management

- Broad line of high quality control products for clinical chemistry, immunodiagnostics, and blood gas analysis
- Blood gas and chemistry data management systems that provide concise, simple documentation for patient and QC records
- QC Systems™ and Confirmation® Services for clinical chemistry and blood gas QC peer comparison documentation

Services that help you meet regulatory requirements

- QC Seminar Program—educates and demonstrates practical implementation of CLIA regulations
- QC Consultant—provides answers to your QC questions in light of the new regulations
- Guidelines to State Operations Manual—lists all guidelines and probes that comply with CLIA regulations
- Calibration Verification Material—verifies calibration of entire patient reportable range for clinical chemistry, immunodiagnostics, and blood gas analysis
- Technical Assistance Center—available 24 hours a day

For an invitation to our next Quality Control seminar and an update on the most recent CLIA regulations, call 1-800-255-3232.

QC Systems™ is a trademark of Ciba Corning Diagnostics Corp.
Confirmation® is a registered trademark of Ciba Corning Diagnostics Corp.

190-12995-A

CIBA·CORNING

Circle 102 on reader service card

RESPIRATION FEEDBACK

The RFb SYSTEM™ retrains diaphragmatic respiration by safely and noninvasively altering brainwave patterns that control this function.

H. Leuner, M.D.

RFb SYSTEM™

• Infrared Diaphragmatic Sensor • Respiration Quotient • Totally Effortless For Patient

"All patients had large improvements in both their 02 saturations and their A.T.S. dyspnea scores."[1]

UNIQUE BENEFITS

RFb ™

• Increases blood oxygen saturation[t]
• Reduces oxygen requirements[t]
• Reduces dyspnea significantly[t]
• Results are long lasting[t]
• Case studies available

"Dyspnea arises from the inappropriate relationship between the force of contraction of the respiratory muscles and the volume of air exchange. It is our belief that RFb realigns this relationship and decreases the work of breathing."[2]

[1,2,t] Wm. Shearouse RRT.
"The Use of Respiratory Biofeedback in Respiratory Disease": Respiratory Care, Nov. 1991.

NO SPECIAL TRAINING REQUIRED
Easy Lease Payments Available
C.P.T. CODE AVAILABLE FOR REIMBURSEMENT

MANUFACTURER REPRESENTATIVE AREAS AVAILABLE

RFB TECHNOLOGIES

5840 Town Bay Drive
Suite #217
Boca Raton, Florida 33486
(407) 367-8611
FAX (407) 451-8560

CAUTION: Law restricts the sale and use by *or* on the order of a licensed practitioner.

Not-for-profit organizations are offered a free advertisement of up to eight lines to appear, on a space-available basis, in Calendar of Events in RESPIRATORY CARE Ads for other meetings are priced at $5.50 per line and require an insertion order. Deadline is the 20th of the month two months preceding the month you wish the ad to run. Submit copy and insertion orders to: Calendar of Events, RESPIRATORY CARE, 11030 Ables Lane • Dallas TX 75229-4593.

Calendar of Events

AARC & AFFILIATES

June 2-6 in Fort Lauderdale, Florida. The FSRC presents the 1992 Sunshine Seminar at the Bonaventure Resort Spa. Topics cover three specialty sections: adult care, neonatal/pediatrics, and management. Also featured are the annual golf tournament, Sputum Bowl competitions, receptions, and banquet. Contact Debbie Herrick at (305) 797-6475.

June 3-5 in St Charles, Illinois. The ISRC presents its 23rd Annual State Convention at Pheasant Run Resort. This year's theme, "Looking Back to Your Future," takes a retrospective and future look at respiratory care. The meeting features lectures, an entry-level review workshop, management workshop, exhibits, entertainment, and a special minisymposium titled "Future Challenges for Health Care Providers." Contact Doug McQuerary (312) 962-4060 or Jane Reynolds (312) 883-6535.

June 3-5 in Checotah, Oklahoma. The OSRC presents its 27th Annual Seminar at the Fountainhead Resort on Lake Eufala. The program features lectures and exhibits. Contact Betty Fisher (405) 636-7065.

June 10-12 in Roundtop, New York. The New York and New Jersey Societies jointly hold their 5th Annual Managers' and Educators' Conference at the Winter Clove Inn. Contact Patty Bowe (519) 270-7454 or Ken Wyka (201) 456-7228.

July 9 in AARC Videoconference. The AARC, in conjunction with VHA Satellite Network, presents "Pulmonary Rehabilitation," one in a series of live satellite videoconferences titled "Professor's Rounds in Respiratory Care." Featured presenters are Drs Barry Make and David J Pierson. Site registration for entire staff is $245 for AARC members. Call (214) 830-0061.

July 15-17 in San Antonio, Texas. The TSRC presents its Annual Convention and Trade Show, "Kaleidoscope of Quality." Featured speakers include Sam Giordano, Dean Hess, Bob Demers, Bob Kacmarek, and Neil MacIntyre. Social events include a barbecue, a 3-K fun run, dances, and an awards ceremony. Contact the TSRC Executive Office, (214) 680-2454.

July 24-26 in Naples, Florida. The AARC's Summer Forum, featuring education and management programs, held at the Registry Resort. For details, refer to the special Summer Forum Program in the April *AARCTimes* or call (214) 243-2272.

October 14 in Auckland, New Zealand. The NZSRC presents its Annual Scientific Meeting at the Aotea Centre. The meeting precedes the Australian-New Zealand Intensive Care Society Conference. Contact Graeme A'Court, PO Box 10148, Balmoral, Auckland, New Zealand, (643) 640640.

OTHER MEETINGS

May 16-23 on a Caribbean Cruise. Come aboard the new Costa Classica for a "Calm Seas Ahead" voyage to Jamaica, Grand Cayman, Cozumel, and Playa del Carmen/Cancun. For information, contact Dream Cruises (714) 636-6660 or 800-462-3628. Write 10882 La Dona Ave, Garden Grove CA 92640.

June 18-19 in Des Moines, Iowa. The Respiratory Care Departments of Iowa Methodist Medical Center and Mercy Hospital Medical Center present the 3rd Annual Respiratory Seminar. Topics include legal issues, ventilator management, post-anesthesia concerns, and updates on airway clearance. Contact Delite Lester, Mercy Hospital Medical Center, (515) 247-4197.

July 29-31 in Salt Lake City, Utah. The Rocky Mountain Center for Occupational and Environmental Health presents "Training for Pulmonary Function Testing," a 2 ½ day course for personnel involved in the performance and interpretation of screening spirometry. Call (801) 581-5710, or write Program Coordinator, Rocky Mountain Center for Occupational and Environmental Health, Building 512, University of Utah, Salt Lake City UT 84112.

September 6-13 on a Caribbean Cruise. Dream Cruises presents its 6th Annual Labor Day Cruise, "Sea No Evil." Ports of call include Miami, Nassau, Blue Island, San Juan, St John, and St Thomas. Starting price with air is $925 per person/double occupancy. Contact Kathy Kearney at 10882 La Dona Ave, Garden Grove CA 92640, (800) 462-3628 or (714) 636-6660.

Notices of competitions, scholarships, fellowships, examination dates, new educational programs, and the like will be listed here free of charge. Items for the Notices section must reach the Journal 60 days before the desired month of publication (January 1 for the March issue, February 1 for the April issue, etc). Include all pertinent information and mail notices to RESPIRATORY CARE Notices Dept, 11030 Ables Lane. Dallas TX 75229-4593.

Notices

The American Respiratory Care Foundation Awards for 1992

Funded by Allen & Hanburys

1. $2,000 for the best original paper (study, evaluation, or case report) *accepted* for publication from December 1991 through October 1992. This award is *not* limited to papers based on OPEN FORUM presentations.

2. Four awards of $1,000 each for papers *accepted* for publication from November 1991 through October 1992 based on *any* OPEN FORUM presentation (not limited to 1991 OPEN FORUM).

3. Five awards of $500 each for the best papers *submitted* (not necessarily published) by 1992 OPEN FORUM participants who have 'never published' in the Journal. The never-published first author must present the abstract at the Annual Meeting and must submit a paper based on the abstract before the 1992 Annual Meeting (*received* in the Editorial Office by November 1, 1992). Co-authors may have previously published in RESPIRATORY CARE.

Funded by Radiometer America

Three awards of $333 each are to be awarded to the authors of the three best features from Test Your Radiologic Skill, Blood Gas Corner, and PFT Corner accepted for publication from November 1991 through October 1992. All three (or none) of the features may be chosen from a specific category (eg, all three may be chosen from Blood Gas Corner).

Registration Reimbursement

As in the past, any 1992 OPEN FORUM presenter (or co-author designee) will receive complimentary registration for an adequately prepared paper based on his 1992 OPEN FORUM abstract, submitted prior to or at the 1992 Annual Meeting.

All awards will be made at the 1992 Annual Meeting. Papers are judged automatically. No application is necessary.

THE NATIONAL BOARD FOR RESPIRATORY CARE—1992 Examination and Fee Schedule

CRTT Examination

EXAMINATION DATE:	JULY 18, 1992
Applications Accepted Beginning:	March 1, 1992
Application Deadline:	May 1, 1992
EXAMINATION DATE:	NOVEMBER 14, 1992
Applications Accepted Beginning:	July 1, 1992
Application Deadline:	September 1, 1992

RRT Examination

EXAMINATION DATE:	JUNE 6, 1992
Applications Accepted Beginning:	December 1, 1991
Application Deadline:	February 1, 1992
EXAMINATION DATE:	DECEMBER 5, 1992
Applications Accepted Beginning:	June 1, 1992
Application Deadline:	August 1, 1992

RPFT Examination

EXAMINATION DATE:	DECEMBER 5, 1992
Applications Accepted Beginning:	July 1, 1992
Application Deadline:	September 1, 1992

CPFT Examination

EXAMINATION DATE:	JUNE 6, 1992
Applications Accepted Beginning:	December 1, 1991
Application Deadline:	April 1, 1992

Fee Schedule

Entry Level CRTT—new applicant:	$ 90.00
Entry Level CRTT—reapplicant:	$ 60.00
RRT Written and Clinical Simulation—	
new applicant:	$190.00
Written Registry Only—new applicant:	$ 90.00
Written Registry Only—reapplicant:	$ 60.00
Clinical Simulation Only new and reapplicant	$100.00
Entry Level CPFT new applicant:	$100.00
Entry Level CPFT—reapplicant:	$ 80.00
Advanced RPFT—new applicant:	$150.00
Advanced RPFT—reapplicant:	$130.00

	Active	Inactive
CRTT Recredentialing:	$25.00	$ 60.00
RRT Recredentialing:		
Written Registry Examination	$25.00	$ 60.00
Clinical Simulation Examination	$65.00	$100.00
CPFT Recredentialing:	$25.00	$ 80.00
RPFT Recredentialing:	$25.00	$130.00
P/P SPEC:	$25.00	$130.00
Membership Renewal: CRTT/RRT/CPFT/RPFT		$ 12.00

8310 Neiman Road • Lenexa, Kansas 66214 • (913) 599-4200

RESPIRATORY CARE • OPEN FORUM

1992 Call for Abstracts

The American Association for Respiratory Care and its science journal, RESPIRATORY CARE, invite submission of brief abstracts related to any aspect of cardiorespiratory care. The abstracts will be reviewed, and selected authors will be invited to present papers at the OPEN FORUM during the AARC Annual Meeting in San Antonio, Texas, December 12-15, 1992. Accepted abstracts will be published in the November 1992 issue of RESPIRATORY CARE. Membership in the AARC is not necessary for participation.

Specifications—READ CAREFULLY!

An abstract may report (1) an **original study**, (2) the **evaluation of a method or device**, or (3) a **case or case series.** Topics may be aspects of adult acute care, continuing care/ rehabilitation, perinatology/pediatrics, cardiopulmonary technology, health occupations education, or management of personnel and health-care delivery. The abstract may have been presented previously at a local or regional—but not national— meeting and should not have been published previously in a national journal. The abstract will be the only evidence by which the reviewers can decide whether the author should be invited to present a paper at the OPEN FORUM. Therefore, *the abstract must provide all important data, findings, and conclusions.* Give specific information. Do not write such general statements as "Results will be presented" or "Significance will be discussed."

Essential Content Elements

An **original study** abstract *must* include (1) Introduction: statement of research problem, question, or hypothesis; (2) Method: description of research design and conduct in sufficient detail to permit judgment of validity; (3) Results: statement of research findings with quantitative data and statistical analysis; (4) Conclusions: interpretation of the meaning of the results. A **method/device** evaluation abstract *must* include (1) Introduction: identification of the method or device and its intended function; (2) Method: description of the evaluation in sufficient detail to permit judgment of its objectivity and validity; (3) Results: findings of the evaluation; (4) Experience: summary of the author's practical experience *or* a notation of lack of experience; (5) Conclusions: interpretation of the evaluation and experience. Cost comparisons should be included where possible and appropriate. A **case report** abstract *must* report a case that is uncommon or of exceptional teaching/learning value and must include (1) case summary and (2) significance of case. Content should reflect results of literature review. The author(s) should have been actively involved in the case and a case-managing physician must be a co-author or must approve the report.

Abstract Format and Typing Instructions

An optical scanner will be used to process abstracts. First line of abstract should be the title. Title should explain content. Type or electronically print the abstract *double-spaced* on *plain white bond paper,* on *one page* only (copier bond is excellent). Do not underline or boldface and insert only one letter space between sentences. Provide a 1-inch margin top and bottom, a 1/2-inch left margin, and an approximate 1/2-inch ragged-right margin. Text submission on diskette is encouraged but must be accompanied by a hard copy. No identification of authors or institutions is to appear on the abstract sheet or within the abstract itself. Make the abstract all one paragraph. Data may be submitted in table form *provided the table width is limited to 55 letter spaces* (ie, letters or numbers plus necessary blank spaces = 55). No figures or illustrations are to be attached to the abstract. Type all information required to complete the author information form on the other side of this page. A photocopy of good quality may be used. Standard abbreviations may be employed without explanation. A new or infrequently used abbreviation should be preceded by the spelled-out term the first time it is used. Any recurring phrase or expression may be abbreviated if it is first explained. Check the abstract for (1) errors in spelling, grammar, facts, and figures; (2) clarity of language; and (3) conformance to these specifications. An abstract not prepared as requested may not be reviewed. Questions about abstract preparation may be telephoned to the editorial staff of RESPIRATORY CARE at (214) 243-2272.

Deadlines

The mandatory Final Deadline is June 6 (postmark). Authors will be notified of acceptance or rejection by *letter only*— to be mailed by August 15. Authors may choose to submit abstracts early. Abstracts received by March 18 will be reviewed and the authors notified by April 24. Rejected abstracts will be accompanied by a written critique that should in many cases enable authors to revise their abstracts and resubmit them by the final deadline (June 6).

Mailing Instructions

Mail (Do not fax!) 1 copy of the abstract, 1 author information sheet, and a stamped, self-addressed postcard (for notice of receipt) to:

RESPIRATORY CARE OPEN FORUM
11030 Ables Lane
Dallas TX 75229-4593

1992 OPEN FORUM
AUTHOR INFORMATION SHEET

Please type:

_____
Abstract title

_____

_____

_____

_____

Principal Author	Institution
Corresponding author	Presenter
Mail station, building, or room	Mail station, building, or room
Institution	Institution
Street address	Street address
City, State, Zip	City, State, Zip
Telephone	Telephone
FAX	FAX
Co-author	Institution
Co-author	Institution
Co-author	Institution

Mail, with abstract and stamped self-addressed postcard, to RESPIRATORY CARE OPEN FORUM
11030 Ables Lane, Dallas TX 75229

New Products & Services

News releases about new products and services will be considered for publication in this section on a space-available basis. There is no charge for these listings. Send descriptive release and glossy black and white photographs to RESPIRATORY CARE journal. New Products and Services Dept, 11030 Ables Lane, Dallas TX 75229.

PORTABLE LIQUID OXYGEN SYSTEM. Companion 550 and 500 lightweight portable systems are designed to be fully compatible with all Companion stationary units. At 5.5 pounds, the Companion 550 is 30% lighter and 35% smaller than the popular Companion 1000. According to the manufacturer, the 550 incorporates an integral demand device coupled with a dual-lumen cannula to provide approximately 8.5 hours of use at 2 L/min in the demand mode and 4.6 hours in the continuous mode; the Companion 500 is the same size as the 550 but does not have the integral demand system and has a conventional single-lumen cannula. Puritan-Bennett, Dept RC, 10800 Pflumm Road, Lenexa KS 66215. (800) 248-0890.

LOW-FLOW OXYGEN REGULATORS. Companion 360 low-flow oxygen regulators are calibrated from 1/32 to 3 L/min, are available in nut-and-tailpiece or yoke configurations for both large and small applications, and are specifically designed for pediatric and transtracheal applications. Puritan-Bennett (800) 248-0890, press 1. Mention RESPIRATORY CARE when you call.

LIQUID OXYGEN BREATHING SYSTEM FOR CHILDREN. Model LOX-C is a 0.25 L liquid oxygen breathing system designed especially for young children. According to the manufacturer, the portable unit (just over 3 lbs when full) can be conveniently placed in a child's backpack, supplies the child with 1-1.5 hours of oxygen, and allows normal mobility. It can also be used effectively by the elderly, especially those with emphysema, and by patients with transtracheal catheters in place. The unit supplies up to 3.5 hours of oxygen when used with a conservation device. Andonian Cryogenics, Dept RC, 26 Farwell St, Newtonville MA 02160. (617) 969-0334.

DRUG DELIVERY SYSTEM FOR MDI. According to the manufacturer, the OptiHaler device improves drug delivery while eliminating the problems of patient timing and inhalation technique, uses a patented aerodynamic design to make the device smaller and more effective than conventional MDI spacers, and directs the aerosol particles away from the mouth then mixes them with a rapidly moving stream of incoming air produced by patient inhalation, which keeps more of the smaller MDI aerosol particles in suspension and allows the larger, less desirable particles to settle out. HealthScan Products, Dept RC, 908 Pompton Ave, Cedar Grove NJ 07009-1292. (800) 962-1266.

LEARNING RESOURCES CATALOG. The 1992 California College Resource Catalog contains educational materials for respiratory care practitioners from student and entry-level to advanced specialists. Featured are "Speaking the Language of Respiratory Care" (audiocassettes and booklet, with a 'talking' dictionary to assure correct pronunciation and definitions) for entry-level students, the Respiratory Care Assistant Course for beginning respiratory care personnel, and the "Flash-Read" speed reading program that includes self-diagnosis and progress measurement for learners at all levels. California College for Health Sciences, Dept RC, 222 West 24th St, National City CA 92050. (800) 221-7374.

SPIROMETER WITH PULSE OXIMETRY. The Schiller SP-200 is now available with S_{aO_2} measurement (saturation and pulse reading complete with waveform on display); with the new option, pulse oximetry is said to be cost-effective and reimbursable. The S_{aO_2} option is also available to current SP-200 users. Schiller America, Dept RC, Suite E, 15461 Red Hill Ave, Tustin CA 92680. (714) 259-9099.

DO-IT-YOURSELF LAMINATOR. The compact model 1200 weighs 6 lbs and allows the lamination of artwork, photos, documents, and ID cards in a preformed plastic film that is sealed on one side to form a pouch. The item to be laminated is inserted into the pouch and then transferred into a carrier; it is then

fed into the laminator where heat and pressure activate the pouch's adhesive coating. No trimming is required; sizes range from 1" × 3 1/2" to 12" × 18", and thickness ranges from 3 mil to 10 mil (comparable to a credit card). The desktop unit itself is 6" high, 3 7/8" wide, and 17" long and runs on house current. The starter kit includes the Model 1200 machine and an assortment of 50 pouches for $199. USI Inc (800) 243-4565. Mention RESPIRATORY CARE when you call.

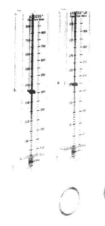

PEAK FLOW METERS. ASSESS Standard and Low-Range Peak Flow Meters meet or exceed all of the technical standards recently issued by an expert panel of the National Institutes of Health and established by the National Asthma Education Program (NAEP). ASSESS performance data include accuracy of ±5%, reproducibility of ±1%, and interdevice variability of ±5%. Accelerated life-span and durability findings project that ASSESS Peak Flow Meters will maintain their accuracy and reproducibility within

±1% for at least two years of daily use. HealthScan Products Inc, Dept RC, 908 Pompton Ave, Unit B2, Cedar Grove NJ 07009-1292. (201) 857-3414.

ATHLETIC DRUG REFERENCE BOOK. Allen & Hanburys Athletic Drug Reference (pocketbook edition) is available for $4.95 plus $2.75 postage and handling (checks, money orders, MC, and Visa accepted). Created to raise awareness of drug education programs and testing policies of the NCAA and the U.S. Olympic Committee, the 280-page handbook includes a question-and-answer section and chapters on anabolic steroids, drug testing procedures, and alcohol use. Clean Data Inc, Dept RC, PO Box 14183, Durham NC 27709-4183.

Authors
in This Issue

Advertisers
in This Issue

Employment Opportunities:

Information Requests or Change of Address

Please complete the card below

AARC Membership No. _____

Old Address

Name _____

Street _____

City/State/Zip _____

New Address

Street _____

City/State/Zip _____

Check the boxes below
for information from the
AARC

❑ Change of address

❑ AARC Membership
Info

❑ AARC Catalog

❑ AARC Position
Statement

RE/PIRATORY CARE

May Reader Service   Expires August 31, 1992

Name _____Ph#_____

Institution _____

Street _____

City/State/Zip _____

Please Circle No More Than 15 Items

80	81	82	83	84	85	86	87	88	89	90	91	92	93	94
95	96	97	98	100	101	102	103	104	105	106	107	108	109	110
111	112	113	114	115	116	117	118	119	120	121	122	123	124	125
126	127	128	129	130	131	132	133	134	135	136	137	138	139	140
141	142	143	144	145	146	147	148	149	150	151	152	153	154	155
156	157	158	159	160	161	162	163	164	165	166	167	168	169	170
171	172	173	174	175	176	177	178	179	180	181	182	183	184	185
186	187	188	189	190	191	192	193	194	195	196	197	198	199	200

I. Type of Instn/Practice
1. ❑ Hosp ≥ 500 or more beds
2. ❑ Hosp 300 to 499 beds
3. ❑ Hosp 200 to 299 beds
4. ❑ Hosp 100 to 199 beds
5. ❑ Hosp <100 or less bedS
6. ❑ Skilled Nursing Facility
7. ❑ Home Care Practice
8. ❑ School
II. Department
A.❑ Respiratory Therapy
B.❑ Cardiopulmonary
C.❑ Anesthesia SeNice
D.❑ Emergency Dept.
III. Specialty
1. ❑ Clinical Practice
2. ❑ Perinatal Pediatrics
3. ❑ Critical Care
4. ❑ Clinical Research
5. ❑ Pulmonary Function Lab
6. ❑ Home Care/Rehab
7. ❑ Education
8. ❑ Management
IV. Position
A.❑ Dept Head
B.❑ Chief Therapist
C.❑ Supervisor
D.❑ Staff Technician
E.❑ Staff Therapist
F.❑ Educator
G.❑ Medical Director
H.❑ Anesthesiologist
I. ❑ Pulmonologist
J. ❑ Other MD
K.❑ Nurse
V. Are you a member of the AARC?
1. ❑ Yes

BUSINESS REPLY CARD
FIRST CLASS   PERMIT NO. 2480   DALLAS, TX

POSTAGE WILL BE PAID BY ADDRESSEE

DAEDALUS ENTERPRISES INC
P.O. BOX 29686
DALLAS, TX   75229-9691

BUSINESS REPLY CARD
FIRST CLASS   PERMIT NO. 604   RIVERTON, NJ

POSTAGE WILL BE PAID BY ADDRESSEE

AARC PUBLICATIONS
P.O. BOX 1856
RIVERTON, NJ 08077-9456

At bedside and during transport, Criticare keeps you informed.

Pulse oximetry engineered for accuracy, versatility and safety.

Criticare's family of bedside oximeters provides accurate information, in a variety of environments, to help ensure patient safety. The 504 series offers unique UltraSync™ software, designed to enhance monitor performance in the active neonate or poorly perfused adult. The 504 series also features trending capabilities, and networks with both the VitalView™ central station and SpaceLabs monitors (through Flexport®).

The portable 503 is ideal for spot checks, transport or continuous monitoring. It's IV pole-mountable, and even performs in the MRI suite.

For more information on how Criticare's proven accuracy* and reliability can support your clinical needs, call **1-800-458-4615**.

CRITICARE
S Y S T E M S, I N C.

Circle 124 on reader service card

Lightning Source UK Ltd.
Milton Keynes UK
UKHW041116290119
336364UK00009B/1696/P